TALES FROM THE ER AND OTHER PLACES

OR

ALWAYS EAT THE LAMB BRAINS!

JEFF WADE, MD

authorHOUSE

AuthorHouse™
1663 Liberty Drive
Bloomington, IN 47403
www.authorhouse.com
Phone: 1 (800) 839-8640

Published by AuthorHouse 10/21/2019

ISBN: 978-1-7283-3169-0 (sc)
ISBN: 978-1-7283-3168-3 (e)

Library of Congress Control Number: 2019916428

Print information available on the last page.

Any people depicted in stock imagery provided by Getty Images are models, and such images are being used for illustrative purposes only. Certain stock imagery © Getty Images.

This book is printed on acid-free paper.

Because of the dynamic nature of the Internet, any web addresses or links contained in this book may have changed since publication and may no longer be valid. The views expressed in this work are solely those of the author and do not necessarily reflect the views of the publisher, and the publisher hereby disclaims any responsibility for them.

This is a work of fiction. All of the characters, names, incidents, organizations, and dialogue in this novel are either the products of the author's imagination or are used fictitiously.

PREFACE

I like stories. And after being an ER doctor for over 20 years, traveling all over, running international medical missions and lately working at a cancer hospital; I've collected many of them. Some of these I have been telling for decades. I think you will like them.

When I first started writing these, I was thinking of one book of travel stories and one of patient stories. As I kept putting them down, I realized most of my stories all could be linked in some way to medicine, even if that was far from the main thing going on in any particular story.

Medicine is one of the biggest parts of my life, but far from the only one. As you will see I have passions for reading, music, languages and travel as well. I hope these varied references & influences make my stories more interesting to read. They run the gamut from interesting, funny, educational, and disgusting to sad or touching. Often several within a single story.

I have passed on a few of these to patients since I have written them. Usually *3 of My Buddies* to patients with alcohol or drug problems who seem receptive. I almost made a guy cry last week doing that. And *Holidays in Cambodia* about meditation and resilience among other things to people who have anxiety &/or depression who are in need of some help.

I would like to take this chance to thank everyone who encouraged me to write, especially Dr. Dang who has been telling me that for about a quarter century. And my wife Lorena for the same but over several less years. And Mordy & Michael for getting me out of the ER and into the cancer hospital where I have had more time and distance to get everything down on paper. And, of course my other family and friends for their support and help with the book and the life.

Mostly I have to thank the patients, students and teachers you will meet through these stories. Some of the, at first, most objectionable ones have ended up becoming important to me. I'm talking about you Betty, Richard, Angus, Rocky, Rosa, Predator and the Hero …

Lastly, I am near the top of the curve in English proficiency. And speak to varying degrees several other languages, and have read extensively. I know how to spell. And I know proper grammar. When I **choose** not to use it, it is for a purpose. These are STORIES after all. They are meant to be like a conversation or if you are listening to a friend tell you a good story. You don't stop your friend in the middle of a juicy story to lecture them about ending a sentence with a preposition. Now do you?

Sit back and enjoy the ride. If all you can do is focus on non-standard grammar or spelling intended to make the story flow better, I didn't do a very good job.

HOLIDAYS IN CAMBODIA

So you been to school for a year or two and you know you've seen it all. In daddy's car thinkin' you'll go far. Back East your type don't crawl. Play ethnicky jazz to parade your snazz on your five-grand stereo. Braggin' that you know how the n*****s feel cold and the slums got so much soul. It's time to taste what you most fear. Right Guard will not help you here. Brace yourself, my dear:

It's a holiday in Cambodia. It's tough, kid, but it's life. It's a holiday in Cambodia. Don't forget to pack a wife. You're a star-belly sneech. You suck like a leach. You want everyone to act like you. Kiss a** while you bitch, so you can get rich. But your boss gets richer off you. Well you'll work harder with a gun in your back for a bowl of rice a day. Slave for soldiers 'til you starve, then your head is skewered on a stake. Now you can go where people are one. Now you can go where they get things done. What you need, my son:

Is a holiday in Cambodia where people dress in black. A holiday in Cambodia where you'll kiss ass or crack. And it's a holiday in Cambodia. Where you'll do what you're told. A holiday in Cambodia where the slums got so much soul.

-*Holiday in Cambodia* by Dead Kennedys

The lyrics to the above song by the '80s hyper-liberal Bay Area shock (as could be guessed by the band name) punk band were probably a mystery to many of the band's fans. For anyone who knows about the history of modern Cambodia, they are a graphic snapshot of life under the Khmer Rouge regime and a searing indictment of spoiled rich (by world standards especially) American kids who think they know real suffering after listening to a few NWA songs. It is simultaneously a sarcastic prescription for breaking out of our cultural inwardness and nationalism that still should be followed today, although I don't recommend traveling to a war zone or genocide site, except for the most daring and committed few, like Doctors Without Borders.

Cambodia at one time was a tropical paradise that was starting to Westernize in its own way. Then came the Vietnam War. As the Viet Cong supported the radical communist Khmer Rouge (red Cambodians) and the US the king, things gradually led to the fall of the monarchy and the dictatorship that eventually killed one quarter to one fifth of the population. All the city dwellers were sent to the countryside to grow rice in areas where it was often not feasible. Outside the communist elites of course—as George Orwell said in *Animal Farm* about a fictitious workers'/animals' revolution: "All animals are equal, but some are more equal than others." Mass starvation, reeducation camps, and the outright execution of 'elites' and 'intellectuals,' which included anyone who wore glasses, tore the country apart. Things got so bad that after the Vietnamese saw what was happening, they sent in their army and kicked the Khmer Rouge out of power despite them both being communists and fighting for their rights and statehood against the capitalist oppressors of the West. Even then it took many years for the Khmer Rouge to be completely defeated, and their successors and those still in power are corrupt and were at one time part of the Khmer Rouge. There are still millions of unexploded land mines littering the country. A paramedic I know spends all his free time traveling there to remove land mines. The country remains one of the world's poorest, with a limited social safety net and poor or absent healthcare. As can be

2

expected, many or potentially most people over the age of forty or so are almost guaranteed have some degree of post-traumatic stress disorder.

I first went to Cambodia with a small group tour of three other doctors all over sixty and my then-girlfriend, now-wife Lorena as we were starting our long-distance relationship going back and forth between Los Angeles and Mexico City as well as various other travels. It was late 2007 and several years after the Angelina Jolie movie *Tomb Raider*, which was partially based in the temple complexes of Angkor Wat in central Cambodia. Angelina truly saved the country. Between the scenes of the far-from-ugly Angie running through the awe-inspiring temples half buried in tree roots in a hugely popular movie based on a hugely popular videogame (the one instance where I think videogames are better than crack) and the publicity raised by her adopting a poor Cambodian child, Cambodia hit the mental map of the West and the US in a big way. Fortunately for her, Cambodia saved Angie as well. She went from being a minor second-generation girl actress known for acting out and marrying the evolutionary throwback Billy Bob Thornton to adopting eighty-four or so children from troubled areas around the world and becoming an UN goodwill ambassador, an adult, and *Angelina* (cue inspiring mood music). By the time we went, Cambodia had become the 'it' location for exotic travel, surpassing the Thai beaches, though it has now been overcome to a certain extent by Burma/Myanmar. Our hotel was one of the best five-star hotels I have ever been in, and there were at least three or four more like it just built or in process when we were there. Things were still pristine and relatively uncommercialized, with many dirt roads between the various temples and tons of monkeys wandering about (one of my personal faves, as I was born in the year of the monkey).

It was there I met a truly heroic man, our guide, Sok.* Sok is about my age, and that meant he was a child when everything hit the fan. He had little chance for a formal education but is very smart and funny an exceptional guide and person. One of his stories/jokes was his reply to a question about snakes. He said there were two kinds

of bad snakes. The first was called the cigarette snake: after you are bit, you have long enough to smoke a cigarette before you die. The second is the two-step snake: after you are bit, you have time to walk two steps.

We first started to learn about his personal history when one of the two older female doctors on the trip (we called them the *abuelas*, Spanish for *grandmothers*) asked him in her endearing, nervous, grandmotherly way if we had to worry about malaria there. His reply was, "No it's not malaria season; now it's fire ant season."

The abuela, of course, followed up with, "Are they very bad if they bite you?"

His reply almost made her tongue fall out of her mouth. "Once I got bit by fire ants and my face swelled up so bad that I could barely open my eyes."

The abuelas asked if that was a normal reaction, and his reply was, "When I was 7, I was torturated (sic) by the Khmer Rouge by being tied to an anthill."

Later we learned his dad had worked with the US during the covert Cambodian side of the Vietnam War. As soon as the Khmer Rouge won, they came to his house and told the dad to come outside immediately or they would blow up the house with everyone inside it. As soon as he got outside, they shot him dead on the doorstep in front of the whole family. A few years later, Sok was made to train for the army, and every child soldier was given the choice of a grenade or a land mine as a weapon. Despite this, he became the wonderful, joyful man that he is today.

*Pho Socheat/speaks English, Italian and Spanish/siemreap@is-cambodia/+855 63 760 282/Indochina Services Cambodia/www.indochina-services.com

One of the abuelas was a psychiatrist, and she asked him if he had any problems after what he went through. He answered that he occasionally had a bad nightmare and woke up screaming, but that was it. Don't get the impression that he was whining or forcing his stories on us—we had to ask him about that stuff. He is the embodiment to me of what has become a popular term in psychology today: *resilience*, also known as the Beethoven Effect. Beethoven was one of the world's best pianists and composers. Music and sound were his life. Then at the midpoint of his career, he went deaf. He lost the ability to play piano or even conduct his own work because he could no longer get feedback to his own ears of how the piano or orchestra sounded. Despite this, he later wrote what is arguably the best piece of music ever, the Ninth Symphony, also known as the "Ode to Joy," based on a poem about how wonderful it is to be alive. You will notice neither of their biographies includes "crawled into a bottle or crack pipe" or "goes to the local ER three times a week when he feels anxious and can't deal with life as it is handed to him" or "has become a psychological/psychosomatic cripple with irritable bowel syndrome, fibromyalgia, and chronic fatigue because daddy didn't buy him a Lexus when he turned sixteen." No one has an answer for why some people are made stronger by what does not kill them, in the words of Nietzsche, and some are killed by it even if they keep eating, breathing, and defecating for another fifty years. Whatever it is, Beethoven and Sok definitely had it.

The temples at Angkor Wat are easily in the top five most beautiful and impressive structures ever built. And they were made while the West was in the Dark Ages. They started out as Hindu temples. During the peak of Cambodian civilization, the king became a Buddhist, and the new ones were built as Buddhist temples. This leads to a wonderful phantasmagoric mix of Hindu myths and Buddhist stories for decoration. Many of the altars are occupied by beatific, shaven-headed, elderly female monks who will say a prayer and tie a yarn bracelet to your wrist in the national colors for a small donation. Wandering around the grounds you are continually impressed by the grandeur and beauty of the temples and the way tree roots thicker than a fat man's torso have woven themselves into and around the man-made temples. All this is untouched as it was lost to all knowledge for hundreds of years and only recently became a tourist attraction.

At least as beautiful and inspiring as the temples are the people of Cambodia. Like Sok, they seem uniformly kind and happy despite their country's history and current reality. Perhaps this is partly due to their strong Buddhist faith and its emphasis on not being overly attached to the things of this world. Perhaps it's because they have more important things to worry about than rush hour traffic and getting a good tax return. They are wonderfully happy and proud that people want to come see their country and its treasures. Food in the finer restaurants is a wonderful fusion of Thai and Vietnamese that has the best of both worlds. One curiosity is the addition of fried crickets, tarantulas, and other vermin to the diet. My understanding is that this started during the mass starvation of the genocide. A cricket or two could easily make the difference between survival and having your head skewered on a stake. Nowadays they are sold outside especially in touristy areas. I both recommend and don't recommend the tarantula. The taste is not exactly prime rib, but did you come all the way to Cambodia to have a quarter pounder with cheese? Really? Really?

My second trip had its genesis over a year before we decided to go. Kaiser Permanente Insurance has a unique type of vertical monopoly where they own several hospitals. If one of their clients goes to a non-Kaiser hospital and needs to stay, they arrange for them to get transferred to their hospital so the money all stays in their pocket and they don't have to pay the price gouging rates normal hospitals charge normal insurance companies before they agree on a more realistic compromise charge. To accomplish this, they have some of their doctors on call answering phone calls from the non-Kaiser ER docs. This is how I met Nak Chhiv. When I asked him how to spell his name for the paperwork, I realized it was Cambodian and said hi and thanks in his language. This led to a conversation about the country and my previous trip there then the sales pitch for his medical mission organization, Project Angkor, which makes yearly trips there to help out. As Kaiser patients always end up in my hospitals and the luck of the draw put me and Nak together for many approval calls, we talked every few months and every time, I got the recruitment pitch. Finally,

I said yes and ended up going with Lorena, now my wife and living together in LA, over new year's 2015.

By then the economy and infrastructure had drastically improved after several more years of the Angelina Effect. There were many more paved roads, the people were noticeably better off especially near the tourist areas, and many more tourist hotels and restaurants. Unfortunately, there are now fewer monkeys and more t-shirt and souvenir stands with hordes of tourists everywhere. Despite the new commercial bustle, the national character is still the same incredible thing. You never feel someone is trying to screw you out of something and you feel like a world class putz if you try to bargain for a lower price on some souvenir. Our guide, so to speak, at the temple area was a very nice man named Visnu (as in the Hindu god Vishnu) we met on the side of the street who drove us around in his little golf cart-like cab. Visiting a few select temples again in a leisurely way was grand and we had a great Cambodian gourmet meal in a hotel restaurant our hotel told us about. They gave us the address and told us it was the Pakkhyat or some such foreign sounding name. It of course ended up being the Park Hyatt and incredible. We ate on a couch around the table and later sat in hammocks outside for a nightcap.

The medical mission trip was several hours away in an especially poor area that was Khmer Rouge territory for years after they were kicked out elsewhere. We celebrated New Year's Eve at a massive outdoor party thrown by the mayor and local government to thank us for helping. Afterwards we set up the clinic and got to work.

Over lunch one day we went to the far side of town to a restaurant we had heard about from one of the Cambodians in our group. On the way there we passed an interesting Buddhist temple and stopped at it on the way back to look around. As we entered, I said hello and thanks to one of the older monks and pretty (all in Cambodian) pointing to the temple grounds. He immediately started calling someone I'll call Augustus. We were all surprised to see a young white guy with an odd affect who didn't really ever make eye contact come out to talk to us. I found out he was from the states, knew Cambodian and was studying to become a Buddhist monk. The first part of the conversation Augustus initiated was 'Do you want to see some bones?' At first, I thought he was a serial killer escaping to Cambodia to try to work through his whole unfortunate habit of killing people then eating their livers with a fine chianti and some fava beans. Now I have been converted to his way of conversation and start all my conversations with strangers with 'Do you want to see some bones?' Augustus truly did take us to a two-story building on the monastery grounds filled both floors from floor to ceiling with bones from the genocide. Maybe a part of Augustus odd mannerisms was from shock at seeing Westerners and attempting to not become overly emotional as part of his monastic training, but I would be surprised if there were not some kind of bad experiences in his past which he was trying to overcome by doing such an extreme change of life and location. I hope he finds whatever he was looking for and that it wasn't my liver.

The clinic we set up was on the grounds of a local hospital but it was far from anything we would imagine as a hospital. As is typical in much of the developing world, the wards have mattresses about the thickness of a sandwich and patients' families are responsible for bringing their food. Minimal X-ray and lab services not to mention medicine is available. We were assisted by local medical students with translation and got to teach and mentor them as well. My first day I had a very earnest sweet innocent girl I will call Vutha. Unfortunately, her English was horrible and she was very tough to work with. I resorted to my Cambodian dictionary to translate to her so she could translate to patients. I talked to Nak the next morning about maybe changing students every day to share the, ahem, wealth around. I was disappointed to see her make a beeline to me to be my translator. She upended my expectations entirely as soon as we started talking, she had looked up all the words she had had trouble with the night before and practiced intensely. Over the next several days I was lucky enough to have her all but one day. She learned what questions and advice I routinely gave and started them before I even got there when she saw which way a particular encounter was going. I am almost certain she saw the first adult penis in her life and career when we had to examine a man down there and I almost had to drag her to the exam room, but she did it. I had brought a special ophthalmoscope to give to one of the students at the end of the trip since I never use it. Vutha truly earned it. She is now the proud owner of one of potentially 5 or less of this particular piece of equipment in the whole country.

As can be expected we could only bring enough medicine to give anyone a month at most of anything and the trip was frustrating in this regard. Acute problems we could deal with pretty well. Of course, a huge percentage of the patients were there for what was obviously anxiety/depression/PTSD, if you asked the right questions and made the right conclusions. What good were a month supply of sleeping pills or valium going to do any of them? I don't even give valium like meds to people in the US, because they have been proven to be highly addictive and make depression and anxiety worse in the long run. The only proven treatments are long term antidepressants, psychotherapy and the dark horse contender meditation (all hit about 30-40% improvement). As I've prescribed meditation to select patients with anxiety and depression over the last several years in the US, I modified this for the local environment. I started out telling them that as they are Buddhists there is a way to get better and that the first truth of the Buddha is that life is suffering, but that everything the Buddha said after that is how to get better. Then I broke down for them the simplest meditation out there: set a clock for 10 or 15 minutes, close your eyes, get comfy and on your first breath in count 1 to yourself, then 2 on the next, when you make it to 10, go back to 1, when you get distracted and realize that, go back to 1 and so on every day. It could be done anytime but maybe best on waking up or to help go to sleep and of course when anxiety is hitting. Then I told them they could also talk to their local Buddhist priest for advice and help in meditating. This really seemed to be useful for many people, definitely better than a few weeks of sleeping pills or valium. In one case in particular the effects were markedly evident. The day before I saw an old woman who fainted and hit her head, possibly from the heat. She was accompanied by her daughter who was freaking out a little making her mom nervous and not helping the situation. Since a CAT scan of her head wasn't an option, we sent her home and had her come back the next day to make sure she didn't have any serious head injury. When I saw them the next day mom's head was fine physically but it was obvious where her daughter had learned her anxious way of reacting to the world. And the daughter was treating her mom almost like a child, not letting her do anything by herself. Some of that is cultural, but this was a grotesque caricature of the typical Confucian respect for your elders. I put them in separate corners and talked to the daughter first about what else was going on. Turned out daughter has HIV and doesn't want mom to worry about her. I told her that she has to let mom do things for herself or it will be bad for them both. Then the Buddhist/meditation spiel I had got down pretty well by then. I added on the advice that that would be the best thing they could do for each other and they could support and remind each other to do it daily, especially when they are feeling bad. By the end of that conversation, the daughter was crying. We then moved on to the mom. We talked over the same things and advice. By the end of that conversation, Vutha and the mom were both crying and my male US medical student and myself both felt a little tugging at the heartstrings. On the last day I sat down with Vutha and told her how she will have a great opportunity and gift being able to do this for her patients for the rest of her career and that she has seen how powerful it can be. Right before I left, I had her give the talk to the people waiting to be seen and promise to do it the last day as well to build her confidence.

I used a variant of this with 2 alcoholic patients. With them I started out saying that as they are Buddhists, this life is only one in an infinite series of future lives and that unless they fix this problem in this life, they will experience ALL the suffering they have had in this life again and again and again. Especially frightening thought for a Cambodian of a certain age. Then the second truth of the Buddha that all suffering is caused by excessive attachment to things, including alcohol. The only way to stop the suffering is to let go (at which point I opened my fist like I was setting something free). Then came the meditation/visit your local Buddhist priest refrain. The older of the guys conveniently didn't make much eye contact and keep looking away at pretty birds or anything else. I am pretty sure he's drunk, hungover or dead by now. The younger guy became very serious and was obviously shaken to his core. I hope he makes it.

A few other people stick out. One was an older well dressed and fed Buddhist monk. He was rather needy, down to the point of asking me to clean the wax out of his ears. I told him how I had been prescribing meditation to several patients and that some may show up to his temple for help. He seemed to be actually irritated that I would be sending people to him for help. Once I saw that, I went big telling him how lucky he is to be able to help his people like this and that that is desperately needed in his country. Don't think he bought it. Oh well, next life he might end up a legless beggar …

Another was a poor 18-year-old kid who had fallen on some electrical transmission wires and lost both hands. He had been in the big city in the hospital for over a month until the day before when they told him they could do nothing else and sent him home. His family brought him straight to our clinic instead. His leg had also been burned and his shin bone was exposed with apparent pus on the surface. We of course could do nothing for him but a single antibiotic shot and had him transported to the big city charity children's hospital. In the West, he could get skin & tissue grafts and keep the leg with a little luck. He probably ended up getting an amputation. What we were able to do for him and many others was provide him with two prosthetic hands. Remember all those land mines. That saved many people from a much worse life, as did our dentists and Nak's mom Nancy, who was an optician and handed out hundreds of pairs of glasses.

My last memorable patient was a beautiful inside and out lady who was crippled from a head injury years before. She was wearing what might have been her only or at least best clothes, pink flannel pyjamas in the tropical heat and the prettiest smile as she limped while in a deep bend at the waist to get around. I treated her for the chronic urine infection she had from not being able to empty her bladder like the rest of us. I also did my standard Buddhist meditation talk to help her deal with her understandable anxiety and depression. And I made it my personal mission to make sure we got her something she could use as a cane to get around. Lorena led her around to the various places like the pharmacy and even one of the edgier staff members felt so bad for her that she gave her $20. Lastly, I told her how happy I was that I could help her and ended telling her in Cambodian that she was pretty and strong and had a pretty and strong mind. Her smile will be with me forever.

DON'T BE THAT GUY!

American Tourist to Moroccan Guy he knows: *I've got to talk to that* (American) *girl over there; can you introduce me to her?*

Moroccan Guy to another local: *Isn't that just like an American? Goes to a foreign country and all he wants to do is talk to other Americans about how hard it is to get a decent hamburger.*

-from *Naked Lunch*, movie based on the book and life of William S. Burroughs

An old friend I met while traveling told me something that really makes a lot of sense: "There are two types of people who travel on vacation: Travelers and Tourists.

My entire Life I have always been a Traveler. I started early in First or Second grade by going to the land of the Sneetches with my first travel agent, Dr. Seuss. The sneetches are kind of like Big Bird from Sesame Street but they come in two types: those with a star on their belly or those without. The Star-Bellied Sneetches got to go to all the cool parties, etc. and those without stayed at home crying in their beer because they couldn't go to the cool parties. One day a con man drove into town and went to the starless losers. He told them 'How'd ya like a star on your belly so you can go to all those cool parties?' They of course said yes. Then he told them 'Now here's what we're gonna do: For five dollars eaches, each one of you sneetches is gonna get into my machine here and when you come out the other side, you'll have a star on your belly.' They did and next day they showed up at the cool party. The original Star-Bellied Sneetches of course said 'What the hell is this trash doing at our party?' He went to those guys the next day and said 'Stars ... So last year's season. No one is wearing stars anymore. Go to the runways in Paris, not gonna see a single star. I would shoot my best friend in the face before I let him leave the house with a star on his belly. Now here's what we're gonna do. For eight dollars eaches, each one of you sneetches is gonna get into my machine here and when you come out the other side, you won't have that scag nasty star on your belly anymore.' And, of course they did. Next thing you know there was this massive feeding frenzy into the machines. Stars on. Stars Off. Money into his pockets. By the time their money runs out, there has been a star on every possible body part. You name it; there has been a star on it. Stars on lips. Stars on asses. Nobody even remembers who had a star or not originally. The last words the guy says as he drives outta town are 'You can't teach a sneetch!' But of course, the sneetches learn to look past star status. This is of course a story with a moral as almost all Seuss' fiction. Appearance, race, wealth, social level shouldn't matter, but of course they do. Maybe Seuss was right, maybe he just had to have a happy ending because it was a children's book. My apologies to my favorite pediatrician Dr. Seuss, by the way. I'm a little hazy on whether the sneetches drank beer and said 'what the hell', but it's been about 40 years since I read the book. We in the West and especially in the United States where the constitution is divinely inspired (Am I right, Jerry Falwell?), are seen by much of the rest of the world as Star-Bellied Sneetches. And too many of us act like the Star-Bellied Sneetches did when the original starless losers showed up at their party. Am I right Donald Trump? This goes quite a ways towards explaining why so many people hate Westerners and Americans in particular and don't necessarily act too friendly towards us when we visit their countries. Even our allies the French can't stand Americans as a general rule.

There is a reason for this. Too many of us might as well be going to the local fake Bavarian village in their hometown rather than really experiencing the local culture and environment. They get in the tourist bus and go to their tourist hotel or boat where they have all their meals, except for the place that is like an Arabian Nights version of the Medieval Times restaurant near Disneyland where you eat period food while watching 20-year-old college students pretend to fight while dressed up like Knights of the Round Table. Or the 'safe for tourists' restaurant for lunch. They get driven to museums and scenic local stuff and are given 25 minutes at each place, maybe an extra 15 minutes if there's a local outdoor market to browse in while tied to the guide's apron strings to make sure they don't get robbed too much, and to get his % later from his friend who conveniently has the best shop in the city. Once the bus trips to the 5 sites of the day are over, they eat the hotel dinner and go to bed early because of jet lag. They learn the 5 words in the local language the guide teaches them by chanting on the bus. They ask questions that you would expect a bright 6th grader to know the answer to about the country. They buy a guide book, but often barely open it on the trip, much less read beforehand. Read books about the country? Or writers from that country? Or novels based in that country? Reading's hard. I'd rather play Angry Birds or watch reality TV or look on Facebook. Even a DVD? Weren't you listening to the last answer? Those would be Tourists. Sometimes known as Ugly Americans. Be comforted though, Ugly comes in all colors and nationalities. And Ugly doesn't have to be a permanent condition. You are reading this after all.

Now who would want to be that guy? We should all try to be Travelers instead. Being a Traveler makes your experience much richer and more meaningful than just being a tourist. The more you know about a country, the culture, the history, the language; the better you will be received wherever you go. The more you learn, the more you will understand and appreciate what you are seeing. The more you prepare for the trip beforehand, the more it can give you. The more outgoing and independent you, are the more you will enjoy the trip. You will have better, more lasting memories to remember for the rest of your life.

The effects even carry over to after you get home. If you learn even a few words and a little about a country, you can meet and have sometimes incredible interactions and conversations with the natives of that country when you get home. I have had fascinating conversations with cabdrivers from all over the world. As driving a cab is not exactly the most glamorous or rewarding profession and requires minimal language skills, cabbies tend to be immigrants. Many of them even have advanced degrees in their home country but can do nothing better here. I usually ask them where they are from, and next thing you know you've reached your destination, had an enjoyable conversation and lightened someone's day by showing interest in and a little knowledge of their home country.

I am an Emergency Room Doctor in Los Angeles. Last time I heard the statistic, there are more people in LA from 14 different countries, than are anywhere else in the world outside their home country. Both at work and out and about in LA, I am constantly bumping into immigrants. Where ever I meet someone, if I ask them where they are from and say a few words in their language it invariably brightens both of our days. I have had many patients who have asked me to be their primary care doctor (not gonna happen since I only work in the ER) because they were impressed and pleased that I spoke a few words in their language and/or expressed interest in their country. Just a few weeks ago an older Jordanian man was so happy that I spoke a little Arabic and had been to and loved his country, that he kissed me on both cheeks at discharge and asked for my card to invite me to his house for a home-cooked Jordanian meal with his family. The call never came, but that's OK. I tend to tell patients the truth and not necessarily sugarcoat it, so if nothing else it helps to reduce the number of complaints I get to my boss if I can talk to them in their language. Not to speak of making my job easier, my patient histories more accurate, the patients feel more comfortable and at ease.

Learning about the country before you go is essential. Do as much as you can. Start preparing for your trip at least 3 months early. A good guide book is the first step. For any country that it is available, the Eyewitness guides are my personal favorite. They have tons of pictures, a good basic history of the country, culture, food, literature and the actual location/site info is very user friendly. Another good supplement is the *insideout* series of pocket size city guides. They fit in your pocket (so make it less obvious you're one of *those* people) and have a fold out map inside each cover. Many are out of print, but Amazon has all. I'm pretty sure they have things that don't even exist. Since they are often out of print, the latest restaurant, etc. info might be a little dated, but are still worthwhile. This is also the time to start on the language. Next is to start getting books on, about or by authors from the area. This gives you a much better background than you can get from the guides and in case of novels is much more fun. If you aren't much of a reader or as a supplement, movies or documentaries about or located in the area are a good option.

It is a whole mindset. Being a Traveler involves more than just preparing before the trip. If you are on a group tour (which I have no problem with, especially as many places are very difficult to get around without a guide, etc.) go with them to all the big places. Keep in mind that you aren't forced to go to anyplace you don't want to. If they are going to another carpet factory tour and you already know how to weave a carpet with your toes after a half dozen similar factory tours, don't go. Sometimes the guides will even try to make a big scene about they have to call the office to see if it is ok. Let them. Usually this is because the factory tours always end in the factory store and the guide or tour company gets a cut. Keep in mind, you paid for this trip, you are in charge. You can always take a taxi (or metro if available) back to the hotel or to someplace else that sounds better. Just make sure you keep the little card with the hotel address to show the cabbie in case he isn't very good at English and ask for a price before you get in the cab. I recommend going to the city center, bazaar/market, or night life area and just wandering around. Find something in your guidebook that they aren't going to, ask your guide, or return to somewhere that you liked from earlier but didn't have time to see as much as you wanted. Even a visit to the mall can be a very different experience from what you are used to and maybe even necessary if your bags are lost or you forgot to pack something.

Never eat dinner in the restaurant in your hotel. It may be 'safer' as far as such things go, but I have gotten Montezuma's revenge more times than I can count from the 'safe' hotel restaurants. Rarely is the hotel restaurant very good, and often it is mostly or even entirely Western food. And just as I wouldn't go to an ethnic restaurant at home where the chef is whiter than I am, I don't recommend eating Western food cooked by someone who doesn't know how to do it the way we would. And did you really travel all that way and spend all that money to eat mediocre versions of what you can get at home? Even if the hotel restaurant has local food, it is rarely that good. Before you get to each new city look in the restaurant section of your guide and plan out a few places. Ask your guide how they are & if he recommends something else. Whatever you decide on ask the hotel staff or guide to call for reservations early. Or just wing it and go to the local bazaar or nightlife area and find something that looks good. If there is a local delicacy or national dish, try it. It will not kill you, and you may even like it. Even the non-hotel restaurants that tour guides take you to are usually full of tourists only and no local would consider eating there. While the food is usually reasonably authentic, it is also pretty unimaginative and not necessarily any safer than anywhere else. Unless it an event-type restaurant (which are often interesting but also can be pretty tacky and inauthentic) or a big going away dinner on the last night, they are usually pretty cheap and not really that special. You are usually better off finding an interesting place and letting the guide know you aren't going to go to the preplanned dinner. They actually like this because they will save the money on feeding you and sometimes, they can even give you a voucher that will cover part of your bill at the new place.

My first time in Morocco, we went to a promising local restaurant walking distance from the hotel that I had seen in our guidebook. The 'salad' course in the Middle East and North Africa has all kinds of little delicacies, very few of which really fit the definition of a salad. On one of the small plates was what looked like 2 rolls of spaghetti. I was a little surprised, but when in Morocco … When I speared one with a fork, it wasn't spaghetti. It ended up being lamb brain. And it was super rich, creamy, buttery. Brains are not something I would ever eat in the US where the slight risk exists to get Mad Cow Disease as animals here are sometimes fed other animals' brains etc. as a cheap filler. In places like Morocco where animals are raised traditionally, no such risk exists. If I had been too squeamish, I would have missed out on a great dining experience. ALWAYS EAT THE LAMB BRAINS!

Take a class if it available. If you are on a cruise or in a resort type hotel, they often offer language classes, cooking classes, native dancing classes, tai chi or yoga. All are a great way to experience more of the culture and learn something you can take back home with you. If you have a smaller tour operator, you can often ask this to be included in your trip beforehand. Smaller boutique hotels can sometimes be talked into giving you a cooking class, even if it's not something they routinely do. A language class is of course something that will be immediately useful for the rest of your trip.

Use the language you are able to learn as much as possible. It doesn't take much to drastically change the way people respond to you. And the more you practice, the better you will get. No one really cares if your pronunciation or grammar are perfect. But they always are appreciated. Unless you are looking to become fluent, pick the most basic language book you can find and maybe a basic cd. We are all children in a new language. Children's language books are excellent for adult learners. The *Your First 100 Words in X* (language) series is usually all you need to get around, shop and be polite as well as other basic needs. They excel in teaching different alphabets (assuming you want to try reading in the language, but reading is not required) or different pronunciation of the letters in ours as well as remembering articles like el or la associated with nouns in languages that have masculine or feminine genders. Many of them are out of print but all can be found from third party sellers on amazon, usually pretty cheap. Just make sure you don't buy a used version as the exercises may already be filled out. If you like CDs better or as a supplement, the *In-Flight X* series is a good start for basics and has a little booklet to follow along. Another nice reference is the *Language Maps* series of laminated folding cards that have essential things in various languages. At minimum, the last several pages of all guidebooks have several pages of common useful words in the local languages. Study it before and during your trip. If you know anyone who speaks that language, practice with them. The least you should learn in any language are the basic polite stuff like hello, thanks, you're welcome, sorry and useful things like how much? where? and expensive. Lastly make an effort to learn how to count at least 1-10, but ideally up to 1000. Once you master 1 through 10; 20, 30, etc. are usually just variations on those words, then you just learn 100 and 1000 and you can bargain!

Speaking of bargaining, JUST DO IT! Almost everywhere in the world outside Western Europe and the US, bargaining is part of the culture and expected. The Chinese, at least, talk of two prices: the sticker price, which the only get from Japanese tourists (they like Japanese tourists even more than we do after the whole Rape of Nanjing thing), and the real price. They look down on the people who don't even try to bargain. In Asia and the Middle East, it is an especially huge thing in the culture. A few shopkeepers will refuse to bargain, but pretty much everywhere outside a mall or chain store, it is fair game. Don't feel bad that you are taking food out of their mouths; they artificially inflate the sticker price to make the compromise price something that will still get them a reasonable profit. If some chump pays the sticker price, they are extra happy, but who wants to be a chump? They will not let you walk out of the store without making a profit. And besides they like the game. Think of it like soccer, everywhere outside the US it is the favorite sport. And once you get into it, you will enjoy the game as well. The first rule is to always try to make your first offer a little less than half the sticker price and ideally almost insulting. If they agree to the first offer and don't laugh in your face, you started too high. For one of my favorite art pieces from Mexico, I gave an initial offer 2/3 of the original because it was very nice and had a moderately big price and got an immediate acceptance. Damn! But it's pretty hard to back down at that point without some major maneuvers and I really love the piece, so it hangs on my wall today. Speaking of maneuvers, use whatever you can think of. If you are with a significant other, do good cop-bad cop and have them pretend to be publicly mad that you are going to spend so much money or to not want it. Also do the slow walk out the door; if they want to make the sale, they are invariably going to say 'wait my friend ...' And their 'last offer' or 'final price' rarely is. If they throw that at you, throw it back at them. Bargaining is a matter of slow incremental raises in your offer until you come to a mutually agreed upon price. They know as a general rule Americans don't have patience for that kind of thing. Use the word expensive in their language and make the offers in their language. If they are a little off balance or impressed from the start, good for you. Some of my most memorable times traveling are bargaining sessions. I have bluffed my way through many bargains by using just a knowledge of the numbers and the word expensive. When you leave you might even get a congratulation from the guide or shopkeeper for a good bargaining job.

A part of not being a Tourist is not looking like one. If they immediately form a bad impression of you, it's hard to get past that. And if there are pickpockets or worse, you don't want to advertise yourself as a Rich (by local standards) Tourist or Infidel. Nearly everywhere outside the US, people dress more formally than we do. The standard Tourist uniform for men and women is a T-shirt, prominent camera &/or passport holder around the neck, shorts (or even sweatpants) and tennis shoes. This makes you a marked man or woman. Shorts may be nice in hot places, but just like Arabs in the desert, loose khakis or something similar are actually cooler and will protect you from mosquitos and sunburn. Many churches, mosques and temples won't even allow you to enter with shorts or a short skirt. Changing clothes on the tourist bus is not very fun or convenient. And often the local culture looks down on showing too much skin anyway. For you ladies, showing lots of skin or dressing too glam can often invite unwanted attention, especially in a country where all the local women are covered a lot more than you. In much of the rest of the world, men are machos and a little sexual harassment or worse is just 'men being men'. A collared shirt for men, even if it's unbuttoned and loose can also help with the sun/heat/mosquitos and make you more socially appropriate. And who knows, you might decide to go to the local gourmet restaurant and have to meet a dress code. The same applies for the shoes. Comfortable dark colored shoes that are good for iffy terrain and easy to take off to enter a temple or mosque are your best bet.

GENERAL TRAVEL TIPS
(A SUPPLEMENTAL MINI-CHAPTER ON ITS OWN)

For starters try to simultaneously travel light and bring anything you might need. The less you have to carry, the less you have to carry. Save some room for souvenirs as well. And keep in mind weight limits are sometimes stricter overseas. Some places will even require you to buy another bag. And even if they don't, extra weight charges can be ugly and slow you down. Maybe even bring an empty cloth bag in case you buy too much. Bring about a week of clothes. If your trip is longer than that plan on using a self-serve laundromat, washing in the sink (if you plan on that bring a few small soap packets, but don't count on that being an option) or just have the hotel or boat wash your clothes when you are getting low. Try to cut out whatever you can. Do have a light hooded jacket in case of rain and warm clothes just in case, unless you're going to the desert in summer. Any medicines you might need should be brought with you, don't rely on getting them there. Airlines sometimes lose bags, so it's best to make plans just in case. Carrying an extra shirt, underwear and socks in your carry-on can't hurt. Also make sure you have at least several days of any medicines you might need and your camera on you, not in the checked bags.

When in a foreign country it is much easier and more accepted to use the local currency in almost all cases. Some places will let you use dollars, but using local money attracts less attention and gives you some souvenirs to take home. As a general rule, if anyone on the street offers to change money, don't. It is often illegal or part of some kind of scam. You may get a better rate, but why take chances? I prefer the local ATMs. The option for withdrawal from your checking account is often called current account overseas. The fee isn't that bad, maybe $5-8 tops from your bank and theirs total. Money changing places or banks also take a percentage and may be watched by criminals. And changing money requires bringing a lot of cash in the first place. Do carry a reasonable amount of cash just in case. Credit cards can't be relied upon as usable at all locations. It is even ideal to have 1 each of MasterCard and Visa in case one or the other is not accepted. Always call the number on the back of your card before leaving the country to let them know you will be out and reduce (but not to zero) the chances you will be denied and have to call to reactivate your card. Some countries are barely hooked up to the international banking system, so you will have no choice but to carry cash. Check with your guide book or travel agent if in doubt.

Despite the horrible sounding movie of the same name, hostels are a valid option. Youth or elder hostels exist. They allow you to have a communal and cheaper experience while traveling that you won't get in a hotel. You may meet other like-minded travelers. My hostel the first time I was in Amsterdam even had a hash bar as part of the facility. You will need to apply online with the international hostel organization before you travel. Along the same line are the cheap traveler's hotels called pension(e)s. All have shared bathrooms outside your room.

Health is always something to take care about and being a doctor, I am well placed to give recommendations, but of course, ask your doctor. The first is vaccinations, any of which should be finished at least 2 weeks or a month before you leave to be most effective. And no, vaccinations do not have any real risk and do not ever give you the disease for which you are vaccinated, much less autism. Just because some brain-dead celebrity with fingers and an internet connection says so, it is not true. This has been scientifically proven in every single legitimate study ever done. The only study that 'showed' harm from vaccines was fraudulent and retracted with sanctions on the doctor who faked the data to prove his point. For starters if it's near flu season, get your flu shot. Sure, they only prevent flu about 2/3 of the time and as low as ¼ of the time in a bad year, but even if it doesn't prevent the flu, it will make the flu less severe. Why take a chance of ruining your whole trip? You might even want to get a Rx of Tamiflu from your doctor if you are traveling at the peak of flu season to take in case the shot doesn't work and you get the flu while traveling. Next up would be hepatitis A vaccine, this is two doses over 6 months, but if you only have time for the 1st, it still works pretty well. Typhoid is a good idea as well. It comes either 4 pills, 1 every other day or a shot. Both are moderately expensive but can even be special ordered and given by your local supermarket or drug store pharmacist, as can almost all my vaccine recommendations. As far as I am concerned, it gives better protection if you do both the pills and shots for typhoid. Area specific for travel to much of South America or Africa is the shot for yellow fever. It may be required to enter the country or to enter another after being in an area with yellow fever. It may be hard to find. The local public health office usually gives it or a travel MD, ask your doctor if he can. Check your guide book on whether it is needed for where you are going. Similarly, the meningitis shot is a light recommendation for desert areas in the Middle East or Africa. Moderately expensive and unlikely, but meningitis will likely kill you or leave you a vegetable if you get it. The same situation applies to the Japanese encephalitis vaccine and travel to South East Asia or India. 1000 people get bit by infected mosquitos and have no problem for every person who gets a serious infection and has their brain turned to oatmeal, but I kind of like my brain the way it is.

Various food and water borne infections are very common in developing countries. No matter how careful you are, it can happen. Best to be prepared. Even better is prevention. Drink only bottled or other purified water and no ice. Try to eat yogurt daily if at all possible, good bacteria might crowd out the bad. If you get the Montezuma's Revenge, stick with clear liquids only for 1 day to let your belly rest and then eat yogurt daily for a few days after you finish the antibiotics to repopulate your good bacteria. About that term by the way, it refers to Montezuma, the last Aztec emperor who was taken captive then killed by the First Ugly American, Cortez. He has gotten his Revenge on this particular white devil more times than I can count. Of course, Revenge comes from many other sources than just Montezuma. I have had Mao Tse Tung's Revenge, Molotov's Revenge (explosive), Mao Mao's Revenge, Mahatma Gandhi's Revenge (surprisingly vengeful for a Hindu pacifist), Machu Pichu's Revenge, Mohammed's Revenge (not surprisingly a wrathful vengeance that involves suffering in the inferno for all infidels), Mongol's Revenge (burns everything to the ground and leaves pyramids of skulls), Myanmar's Revenge (vengeance with the full force of a military dictatorship) and Mekong's Revenge. Currently the best overall option is Zithromax 1 gram once as soon as the diarrhea starts. It often makes you drastically better in just an hour or two. It might even be best to get a Rx from your doc for Flagyl 500 milligrams 3 times a day for 3 days in case that doesn't work. Depending on how many people are going and how long you are going for, you should ask your doctor for several doses of the 1st and a few of the second. Different species of lightning diarrhea bacteria can strike twice or more on a trip.

Malaria is another concern in the tropics. Again, prevention is best. Long sleeves and pants and frequently applied insect repellent work pretty well. Even if you are taking antimalarial pills, that doesn't prevent Dengue or Chikungunya or even weirder mosquito borne infections and they aren't 100% guaranteed to prevent malaria. You can look on the Center for Disease Control website to see whether antimalarial pills are recommended for your area:

http://www.cdc.gov/malaria/travelers/country_table/a.html.

Also look in your guidebook or ask your travel agent. The best overall option is Malarone starting 1-2 days before you go and for a week after you leave. It covers all the possible types of malaria and has the least side effects with the easiest dosing.

Since stuff happens, also take some other precautions. Make extra copies of your passport and itinerary with hotels and contact info and put one in each bag or carry-on. Send all your family a copy of your itinerary, etc. as well. You can buy a reasonably priced satellite phone from mobal.com, which will work almost anywhere and then you only pay per call after. US based cellphones may work on a country by country basis. Check with your provider beforehand if there are any additional options you can buy to make your cellphone work. You can also buy a new SIM card for your phone at the airport or other places in your destination to make cheap local calls and use the local cellular service for data. It will temporarily change your # to a local one and make sure it has sufficient phone and data preloaded. At minimum a smartphone will be able to do email, WhatsApp, Skype and Facetime in areas with Wi-Fi. If you are going anyplace dodgy it would be a good idea to register your trip with the state department which gives you extra travel alerts and help in case something bad happens at: https://step.state.gov/step/.

Lastly, I recommend travel insurance as well. Not only will they pay for the trip if you can't go for some reason, they cover lost bags, and provide you medical insurance. The last point makes it all worthwhile as almost all US insurance is useless overseas. I had to cancel a trip at the last minute due to emergency eye surgery and got all my money back. And speaking of stuff happening, it never hurts to bring a roll of travel size toilet paper.

One last thing, passports and visas can get a little tricky. Most places require you to have 6 months left before expiration of your passport when you enter the country. Visas are needed most places outside Western Europe, Mexico and Canada. Some may take up to 2 months for approval and return of your original passport with the visa. Always check if a visa is needed with plenty of time to get it before you travel. Wikipedia has a page on visa requirements for US passport holders. I have used and recommend Washington Visa and Passport Services (wvps.com) many times and they are excellent. They are in DC where most embassies are, have extensive history with all the countries and great customer service. Some of the more paranoid countries are best to have your travel agent arrange as there are many supporting documents and tricky applications. Some countries like Cambodia and Myanmar/Burma even allow you to apply online and print your visa or pre-approval letter at home without sending your passport anywhere.

4 OUT OF EVERY 5 DENTISTS RECOMMEND SUGAR FREE GUM

-classic chewing gum commercial from the '70s

Smoking is just plain dumb. 5 out of every 5 doctors will agree with you there. And one always has to wonder about that 5th dentist in the quote above who *doesn't* recommend sugar free gum. Did he go to dental school through the mail? Is he the Dick Cheney of dentistry who wants his clients to get more cavities so he gets more business? Just like Cheney who pushed for the invasion of Iraq & conveniently enough owned Halliburton that helped clean up the mess in the oilfields afterwards.

Thanks to the massive awareness of smoking's dumbness it has got pretty unpopular and fewer people smoke nowadays. This is a great thing for everyone but the tobacco companies. Also, a great thing for everyone's tax dollars as millions of Medicare/Medicaid $s are spent on smoking related illnesses. Now however, it has taken on a new form, **vaping**. Nicotine is vaporized and inhaled with a bunch of other chemicals, often including fruit and candy flavors. Conveniently enough kids are attracted to those flavors. And not too long ago, the FDA made it illegal to sell flavored cigarettes for this exact reason.

The false prophets of vaping will tell you it's so much safer than smoking or even completely safe. It won't give you cancer or emphysema, it doesn't smell, it burns the lungs less so they feel better breathing, it won't cause second hand cancer or emphysema …

I call bullshit on that.

Nobody has really had a chance yet to see what inhaling these chemicals and flavoring agents might do to you 20 or more years from now. It *has* been shown in a few case studies to cause this weird immune reaction to the lungs even after only a few times vaping. This could even end up being fatal if untreated. And just like any high-powered small battery, they can explode with no warning. Especially nice if you carry it in your pants pocket ... They are even more prone to explode when in use. One case I read about sent the mouthpiece straight through the back of the guy's (and just like alcohol, drugs and crime, the #s are way in favor of it being a guy) throat and into his spine. And there are dozens of cases about exploding batteries. Even the no second hand smoke thing still doesn't fly, because no one knows the risks of second hand vapor yet either.

But there's a bigger problem with vaping, you are still inhaling nicotine. Nicotine is still a dangerous drug. You are still actively indulging in a nicotine addiction. And because it is 'safe' and less stinky and if you are a child (or childish, & I believe a strong case can be made for anyone who still smokes in this day and age being childish at some level) it tastes like candy; it is much more acceptable. Smokers are being encouraged to vape instead. And kids who think smoking is disgusting are doing it to be cool &/or get a nicotine high.

This means the same risks that go with any other form of nicotine: heart attacks, strokes, losing feet due to poor circulation, impotence, more chance to start using alcohol or other drugs and less chance to stay off them as long as you keep shoving nicotine into your system multiple times a day. Sign me up!

Unfortunately, when you look at the overall statistics for smoking the picture looks pretty grim. About 90% of people who smoke drink to some extent. Likewise, 90% of alcoholics and drug addicts smoke. The dumber you are (IQ and level of school completed), the more likely you will smoke. If you are schizophrenic, there is a 90% chance you smoke. Similar but somewhat lesser %s of bipolars or people with severe depression smoke. If you are in jail there is a 90% chance you smoke. The lower your income, the more likely you smoke. And the lower the socioeconomic status of your parents, the more likely you smoke.

Not exactly the people you would expect to quit nicotine entirely or realize that the gospel of vaping is bullshit. And I tend to think a lot of the above statistics are all related to an inborn &/or learned tendency to bad judgment or lack of will power. The same guy who thinks smoking is cool & likes the high, is more likely to treat alcohol and meth and coke and heroin the same. And to not have the stick-to-itiveness to quit. The same could be said for crime. Mental illness is at least partly a matter of judgment. The same guy is also likely to be without the willpower to get a degree or work in a crappy job until he gets to be a manager, etc. And they probably come from a house with parents who smoke (and had similar judgment & willpower) which they passed on to their kids by genes or example. Not to mention that it is so much easier to smoke as a minor when you can sneak them from your parents' stash.

Anyway, a few of my co-workers started vaping. One is almost definitely an alcoholic, sometimes not a very functional one at that. Really cool, nice, overall good guy who never smoked. One day I went out to get my car to get something in the middle of a shift and noticed him hanging out with the smoking/vaping lunkheads. And this guy was sucking on a vape stick! When I asked him about that, his reply was: 'It relaxes me'. Mine was: 'So would heroin & I don't recommend that either' as I walked away shaking my head. Not surprising in retrospect.

The other guy is actually a doctor and I suspect a functioning alcoholic to tell from his stories. And nobody with any sense tells people they work with the full truth of their drinking/partying, so ... Of course, he smoked. Then he switched to vaping. I, of course, always gave him a hard time about it.

One day I came up with an inspiration while driving into work when I knew he was on. Once I got settled in, I told him: **'I prefer my heroin using patients to use clean needles and sterile heroin, but I much prefer them to stop shoving heroin into their veins!'** He didn't have much to say to that. And of course, he still carries his vape stick around with him like Linus from *Peanuts* carries his blankie ...

3 OF MY BUDDIES

"Straight Edge"

I'm a person just like you
But I've got better things to do
Than sit around and f*** my head
Hang out with the living dead
Pass out at the shows
Always gonna keep in touch
Never want to use a crutch
I've got the straight edge

"Out of Step"

I don't smoke
I don't drink
I don't f***
At least I can f***ing think
This is no set of rules
Because of these things, whether they're, whether
they're f**king or whether it's playing golf
I feel that …
Out of step, with the world!

-2 songs from Minor Threat

The above lyrics are from the 'straight edge' hardcore punk band Minor Threat. Straight Edge is a subclass of the punk scene. They don't believe in or use drugs (including nicotine), alcohol or promiscuous sex. This literally set them out of step with most of the rest of the punk scene, not to mention society at large. Minor Threat fans tended to be pretty politically correct and extreme. More than 1 person was beaten up at their shows for smoking pot or drinking. Nonetheless, it is a much healthier way of life than that followed by most people.

As an ER doctor, I see alcoholics every day. Either brought in because they fall down or just because they are passed out and some concerned bystander calls 911. There is a famous ER doc who tells a (true) joke when he lectures all over the world. I will tell it as he does to make it work better: 'I always ask the med students why alcoholics get so many bleeds in the brain. And they come up with some good sh** these students do. Their brain shrivels up because they use it for nothing but drinking, the skull doesn't. Brain rattles around in big empty skull, boom, bleed. They get cirrhosis so the spleen swells to the size of a basketball & breaks down all the clotting cells, boom, bleed. Cirrhosis again, liver doesn't make clotting proteins, boom, bleed. Bone marrow stops making clotting cells, boom, bleed. Balance off, boom, bleed. But these students always miss the #1 reason why alcoholics get bleeds in the brain, THEY ARE DRUNK AND OBNOXIOUS SO PEOPLE WANT TO HIT THEM!' But seriously, alcoholism kills and kills relationships.

I always stick to the harsh facts when I see drunks in the ER. 'When's the last time you went to AA? When's the last time you drank &/or used? You have to get to AA daily for the foreseeable future & people who want to live go 2-3 times a day the first month or so. If you don't you will be dead soon. And it will be alone and ugly.' If they already have cirrhosis, I tell them 'You could easily be dead before 6 months, if you keep this up.' This is the only intervention proven to work. Of course, it is not perfect, but drinking instead of AA is proven to fail. When I send them home, I repeat it until they give the right answer. 'Where are you going tomorrow?' 'AA.' 'And the day after that?' 'AA.' 'Or?' 'I will be dead soon.' Of course, I still see the same people again & again & many never get it. Three however actually have.

'Richard' would sometimes come in twice a day drunk. When he was drunk, he was a whiney needy little bitch. When he sobered up one morning, he actually paid attention. The next time I saw him he was there with his mom who was a patient, clean & upright. He told me that he had gone to AA & talked to his dad who had a similar issue when he was younger. I saw him drunk again a few months later & we had the same talk. The next time I saw him, he was there as I came in and was visiting his mom who was a patient again. He came right up to me and gave me a big bear hug which shocked the hell out of the day doctor. Last time I saw him, he was drunk again. When he sobered up, he was feeling like an idiot so I spent a lot of time making sure he knew everyone screws up sometimes and he just needs to start again. **He** made sure he got out in time for his regular am AA meeting.

'Angus' is half deaf from playing drums in various speed metal and punk bands when he was younger. And has chronic pancreatitis from drinking. Someday it will kill him, if it hasn't already. One day when he was nearly sober and after the nurses coincidentally mentioned his deafness and the cause, we had a long talk. I asked him if he knew Minor Threat and more importantly WHAT they were. We had a long talk about how he needed to become a straight edge or die soon. I even printed the above lyrics and let him use his headphones to listen to the songs from my phone. From that moment he idolized me and, unfortunately got much worse in his drinking. I don't think I ever saw him sober when he came in again. Every time, I told him he needed to become a straight edge or a dead one. Last time I saw him, we ended up in the cafeteria together in the morning. He told me how he was living in someone's body shop garage and had lost everything. And that I was his only friend. I told him that if he got into AA regularly, he could develop new friends and get his life back. I then made sure the nurses got him some clean clothes. That was the last time I saw him. I hope it was because he sobered up. I fear the worst however.

'Robbie' was a longtime heroin addict, smoker and alcoholic with hepatitis C from using needles that had already caused cirrhosis. It has always been my opinion if you were an adult male and you used a childish version of your name that ends in '-ie', you were not likely to truly be an **adult** male. He could be a real jerk to the nurses if they were 'soft,' pushing them for more pain meds, etc. I know everyone is shocked that a drug addict could be jerky. I however am not soft. I always read him the party line, while listening to him and his stories of living in a storage unit because his wife kicked him out again. I of course used that to turn it back to his using was the reason for the problems in his life. And made sure he knew that he went to AA & got sober or he would quit using, soon, the 6 feet under way. I never saw him with his family that I remember, not surprisingly. Because I was firm but honest and gave him a way out, he really became fond of me. And had several long episodes of sobriety. When he came in and saw me, his face would light up & he would shout out 'there's my doctor!' I think the last time I saw him he had fallen off the wagon again but said he was going back to AA, etc. Then he kind of hurried out of the ER. Last week I got a call when I was in the breakroom. The nurse told me 'A Sara Tomas wants to talk to you; she said her husband died.' This summoned visions of being screamed at for 'killing' somebody and threatened with a lawsuit. My heart was racing a little when I picked up the phone. It was Robbie's wife. She wanted to let me know that he had just died. Apparently, he had told her several times about me and what I had told him. It was quite a blow to me as I really had gotten to like Robbie despite his flaws. I comforted her as much as I could and suggested she might try Alanon, the sister program of AA intended for family members of alcoholics. She thanked me for trying to help him.

A SHARP DRESSED MAN

God and the Devil make a bet. They bet about whether or not they can make this guy Job turn against God by taking away his wife, kids, money, health, etc. They take away everything he has and inflict him with painful sores.

When they go back to see who won the bet, of course God won & Job is still praising him. He did write The Book, of course. Haven't seen the Devil's version yet …

God then gives him a new family, etc.

-the Book of Job, Old Testament

'Job' is another special guy. He seems to be homeless. He also cross-dresses every day. This is not the best combo plate. He has supposedly been beaten up several times because of the way he dresses. Shelters are not a safe option for him. Especially when you consider they are largely full of alcoholics, drug addicts and people with psychiatric issues. They aren't exactly the safest people to be around when you are not a late 50s black man wearing a dress.

Job takes pains with his appearance. He wears a full length semi-formal dress. He stuffs some tissue in the chest to fill it out. He is not effeminate at all aside from being very soft spoken. I doubt he is gay or anything but just plain Job. He keeps his hair kinda bushy and uncombed and doesn't wear makeup, so he stands out. He has some kind of neck problem so always carries his head deeply tucked down. He is unfailingly polite, never really asks for anything and always says please and thank you.

He is such a sweet kind guy that it is hard not to feel sorry for him. He also seems to have some form of mental illness. His stories just don't seem to check out. And he likely has some mild-ish mental retardation. That would explain his child-like innocence. He talks about how he sings in the choir at a local church. Whenever I have asked him which one, the details never seem to arrive. When I ask him about his favorite song the answer comes very slow and not very fitting. When I have asked him to sing for me, he can barely bring out a line or two.

I have actually seen him walking around town several times. Once I was able to stop and talk to him. He didn't seem to recognize me but told me how he was getting cataracts taken out at Hospital X soon. He was energetic and talkative within his limitations and seemed to enjoy that someone knew him and wanted to talk to him.

Because it literally is not safe for him on the streets at night, he stays in an ER lobby every night. He usually says that he has some kind of vague minor pain or stomach ache and gets some Tylenol or Maalox then sleeps in the lobby the rest of the night. At my main ER, he was coming in so often that administration told the registration clerks to call the Social Worker when he came in to see if they could place him somewhere. Once that happened, he just stopped coming there at all. I assume he is wary of those people because he doesn't like being put somewhere.

Then he started coming to my other ER (a 20 or more-minute drive away) every night. I made it my ritual once I knew he was there to bring him some food, juice and a blanket. I would also spend some time talking to him and asking how he was doing. Then I would ask if he really wanted to be seen by the doctor or just needed a place to stay for the night. Rarely did this seem to stop him from asking for a formal, expensive ER visit at the taxpayers' expense, but I'm OK with that.

He needs more people who care for him. I decided to compliment him one day by calling him a Sharp Dressed Man (as in the ZZ Top song). It is true and he can use that kind of input. I'm sure he doesn't get much along those lines.

Just like the biblical Job, my Job is always happy and still goes to church regularly. Many people dealt much better hands in life are not as happy with their lot as he is.

We could all stand to be more like Job.

AIN'T NOBOODY GOT TIME FOR THAT

Some people are just cheap dates.

-one of my life lessons

Back in residency at MLK hospital in Compton I saw one patient who 'taught' me the above lesson about human behavior. Keep in mind that it doesn't take much to barely get by if you don't mind living in a bad neighborhood, not having nice stuff and not going anywhere fun. State Social Security Disability Income back then was about $800 a month. Some people have such low expectations that they are willing to get by on that if it means they don't ever need to work. I see the same phenomenon in repeat offenders who are in the ER to get a quick medical checkup before going back to jail again. Too many of them don't care that they are going back to jail. It's easier than working instead of doing crimes. And the psych patients who know that if they say the right thing, they can get a psych hospital bed for 3 days by telling everyone who doesn't want to listen that they are suicidal for the 5th time this month. Definitely easier than actually committing suicide ...

I see the same thing with drug seekers as well. A rare subculture of the drug addict community will go from ER to ER faking a muscle spasm from anti-vomiting or antipsychotic meds. The cure for this common side effect is Benadryl, the allergy medicine or sleeping pill. It is a mild sedative and works stronger and faster if it is given in an IV shot, as it is for those people with the medication side effect mentioned above. Regardless, not very exciting stuff, but for some people, that floats their boat. Not nearly as fun as real narcotics, but a hell of a lot easier to get. I bet those guys' idea of a good date is McDonald's $1 menu and reruns on broadcast TV.

This patient was a young guy under 25 with a badly broken hand or foot. It would need surgery to ever work right again. I saw him and told him we would admit him to the hospital to get surgery to fix it.

He refused surgery and requested to sign out Against Medical Advice. I tried to convince him that he needed surgery if he ever wanted to use his hand or foot right for the rest of his life.

Once he heard that, his eyes lit up like the kid in *Charlie & the Chocolate Factory* when he got the golden ticket.

He looked up at me and said 'You mean I can get disability?'

He walked out of the hospital shortly after and took a huge chunk of my faith in humanity with him.

AM I IN THE RIGHT ROOM?

K hole: Noun. To have used too much of the drug ketamine (special K) and lost sense of time and space, balance, verbal skills.

-Urban Dictionary definition

Ketamine is a weird drug. It is called a dissociative anesthetic. In English, that means it helps pain by making it an impersonal experience. You know you have pain, but the ties between knowing you have it & feeling it emotionally/suffering from it are cut. With higher doses this can cut all your ties with the outside world. It apparently feels like you are falling down a dark hole. It is also a heavy-duty stimulant. To the point you can easily get a stroke or have your heart or breathing stop. And has a narrow window of a safe dose. And is infamous for emergence reactions. Again, in English, that means you can freak out when you come around with hallucinations and paranoia. Many docs will give a little of some valium like stuff with it to prevent that.

It is a close relative of PCP/angel dust. PCP is a very messy drug. The hallucinations and paranoia are even worse than with its cleaned up pharmaceutical cousin. Also, since it is both a stimulant and anesthetic, people can get very violent & be nearly impossible to take down. They don't even notice that the cops have just blown their hand off with a .45. It is such a strong stimulant that it raises the brain chemicals exactly like they are in a schizophrenic during a bad psychotic break. Nice. And some people like that. Go figure.

Fortunately, due to its bad side effects, it has gotten pretty unpopular, despite a brief comeback a few years ago.

Not too long ago K was the cool party drug. The popularity for a drug of abuse has waned since then. More scarily, it is now getting lots of medical props and use for the more unusual effects. It is being used for chronic pain. And has been shown to cause improvement in depression that lasts several days after a dose. Maybe it's kinda like electroshock therapy in that it releases so many neurotransmitters at once it causes a seismic shift in your mood, etc. It is being used as a second line pain medicine in some hospitals. More ominously, various at least slightly shady docs are setting up ketamine clinics where you can pay a ton o'$ and get hooked up for a half hour for your pain or depression then go home. That sounds safe, don't it?

My buddy 'Andrew' was Samoan, but he didn't look it. He looked more like a dark skinned latino with kinda bushy black hair and beard and funny, sad eyes. His last name wasn't very typical Samoan/ Hawaiian either. Not something like Manolilipolani or whatnot. It was a 2-syllable name that looked closest to a slightly offbeat Chinese name.

I met him at work 6-9 months ago. I saw his name and went to his room expecting to see a Chinese guy & maybe rap a little in Chinese. When I opened his curtain, I saw Andrew instead. I quickly said sorry and went back to the board to make sure I was in the right room. When I went back, I told him about that & asked him where the name was from. He said Samoa, so I said my one word in Samoan, **talofa**, which is related to the Hawaiian word aloha & means hi or bye. He laughed and got a huge beatific smile on his face. Then we dealt with his medical issue. I saw him several more times after and we always told each other TALOFA!

One nite they called for a Rapid Response Team (RRT). Kind of like calling for a code blue, but not as severe. When I got there, it was Andrew. He had just got his first dose of ketamine ever. And his nurse has a reputation for slamming the meds in fast to save time. Big mistake. He had at first collapsed & by the time I got there was agitated & shouting 'What? What's going on? Etc.' Once I got the

41

story, we go him some valium-y stuff and he mellowed. As soon as he came around, he said: "TALOFA!" to me. I explained to him and his wife the whole K hole thing and he never got that medicine again. But the pain from his cancer kept getting harder to manage. I kept seeing him again as a patient semiregularly & we reminisced about his bad K hole experience. When I would see his name on the board, I tended to stop in for a few and say talofa, even if he wasn't my patient at the time.

Last nite I got a call from one of the ICU nurses asking me for a favor. A patient had just passed away & the family was upset but the doctor for that side of the hospital was busy with someone who was still breathing elsewhere so couldn't make it. She asked me to come talk to them as a favor. She is a very good, nice nurse & I try to be helpful as a general rule, so I went even though I was very busy myself.

When I got there, I saw a guy outside the room & the doors & curtain were closed. As soon as I got in the room, I saw that it was Andrew. and my heart sank. I went back out and collected the brother (?) to go to the lobby and get the rest of the family. We then all went in and saw him together. I said the standard stuff about he is out of pain now at least and has had a very tough last several months. Except for his wife, I didn't know any of the rest of his family, but we explained some of our shared history to them. I said it was sad that I wouldn't get to tell him talofa anymore. I gave his wife a hug and told her I was sorry and a brief one to his brother. Before I left, I put my hand on his chest and told him 'Talofa my friend.' with a little catch in my voice and almost tearing up a little.

I am glad I got to be there for his life and death. As I told the other doc on that nite, it was for the best that I ended up being the one who went since I had history with them.

TALOFA MY FRIEND!

BOBA STONE

boba: Noun. Small, usually black, balls of tapioca used in beverages, which are generally consumed through a large straw. A beverage containing these balls of tapioca.

-Wikipedia definition

Cerebral Palsy (CP) is a horrible disease. Usually during a difficult labor, not enough oxygen gets to the baby's brain and they are left with permanent brain damage. Even worse (in some ways), they are often, if not mostly, intact mentally. Unfortunately, they don't look like it. They usually have some problems talking and moving some part(s) of their body. Often, they have these slow, repetitive twitching motions of their hand(s). Some people are so affected they can't walk, talk or take care of themselves at all. And if you look 'retarded' people tend to treat you that way.

A friend of mine from high school had CP. He was a great, nice kid who read books for pleasure on his own doing. He also didn't look or talk normal, so wasn't very popular. His sister (crappy luck for his folks) also had CP and was much worse.

Because of him, I've always had a soft spot for people with CP. If you know what to look for, the diagnosis is obvious. If I am traveling and see someone with it begging, I always give them (for the local area) a very big amount of $. And am extra nice to them.

One day the ambulance brought in a guy from a nursing home with CP and belly pain for a few days. He was bed bound and unable to talk at all. Since we couldn't get any story from him, we started blood tests and were about to put in a catheter to get some urine. The nurse called me in to see something that was just at the tip of his penis. It turned out to be a kidney stone. When it came out, his urine fountained out for quite a while afterward as it couldn't get past the stone for days. The stone was the size of one of those little tapioca balls called boba that (at least in the new Chinatown area of LA) are so popular in various tea or coffee drinks. About as big around as your fingernail for those of you in the Midwest. But, unlike the chewy tapioca balls, kidney stones are hard as rocks.

Kidney stones are supposedly the worst pain you can have. Dunno how they came up with that factoid, but they definitely are not fun. All the urine on one side gets backed up. Think of the last time you had to pee really bad & couldn't. And when you stretch any organ muscle (like in the tubes between your kidney and bladder), they contract in a reflex. This raises the pressure & the pain. Most are less than an eighth of an inch across. Ones over a quarter inch are typically unlikely to pass on their own & a urologist needs to put a camera up to pull them out. Even more fun.

This poor guy had a huge stone for days. And couldn't do more than look pained and point at his belly. And as most nursing home staff are lazy, stupid or incompetent until proven otherwise, it took days for them to call an ambulance to get it taken care of. Fortunately for him, they eventually realized they could watch more TV if they called an ambulance. Then it went to his bladder and later penis. At this point he went from pain from urine not being able to get out of one kidney while more urine is constantly being made, to it not being able to get out of his bladder or either kidney. Poor guy.

You should've seen the look of relief on his face when the stone popped out and the fountain of urine commenced.

As a personal aside, I swore off boba years ago. They aren't that tasty or interesting to chew. And since I work in the new Chinatown of LA, I have had so many boba, that towards the end of my boba days anytime I went to the bathroom (sitting or standing) nothing came out but boba ...

CIRCLING THE LIQUOR AISLE

Theft of expensive liquor from bottle shops is a problem
that is reaching epidemic proportions. With the EasiCap
security bottle caps from Retail Theft Control, liquor theft
can be a thing of the past. Each cap is made from almost
indestructible polycarbonate and contains an EAS tag.
The fully enclosed design prevents the decanting of the bottles
in the store.

-literature from the website of the Bottle Cap anti-
theft device which you find attached to most bottles
of liquor in your local supermarket

I went to residency at Martin Luther King Hospital in South Central
Los Angeles, so just like the seminal rap group NWA (I believe it
stands for Negroes With Attitudes …), I am Straight Outta Compton,
yo. As the comic Chris Rock says: 'Wherever you go in this country,
if you end up on MLK Boulevard. It's probably not in a very good
neighborhood.' South Central LA had such a bad reputation that
the City formally changed the name to South LA. The day after the
name change, the neighborhood went from majority poor blacks and
Latinos to exclusively white studio executives. All the drugs, crime
and prostitution disappeared and it became a paradise on Earth.
Right … But the name change stuck, shows that bullshit works.

One of the local denizens was an abusive, manipulative drunk
guy with one good eye. He also used a wheelchair because he was
partially paralyzed in his legs. He could get around slowly and poorly

if he wanted to when he was halfway sober, but he preferred to have everyone serve him. The chair and the eye probably increased his take at panhandling of course as well. But knowing how much of an ass he could be, especially but definitely not exclusively when he was drunk, I am sure there was a good reason for both problems that didn't truly merit anyone's sympathy. As the song says: Blame it on the alcohol …

One of my first jobs after graduating was at a hospital that was at the top of a hill. At the bottom of the hill was a traffic circle and across from that a local chain supermarket. Fortunately for me, this guy graduated from MLK the same time as I did and followed me to the hospital on the hill.

He quickly fell into a pattern. He would come in drunker than shit, usually covered in his own shit (appropriately) &/or piss with a blood alcohol 3-4 times the legal limit to drive. Then sober up after several hours of being nasty and get discharged. He would get in his chair, point it downhill, go to the supermarket, head straight for the liquor aisle and open the biggest bottle of liquor he could find and chug it right there.

When he got taken back to the ER, his alcohol level was back at his standard.

Then repeat.

And repeat.

Groundhog Day of drunkenness.

This guy (and his many friends under the skin) is why you can't buy a bottle of liquor in a big store nowadays without having the clerk remove the big extra cap after you pay for it.

CLITORIS

Clitoris: noun. A sensitive elongated erectile organ at the anterior part of the vulva in female humans and mammals, homologous with the penis. Supposedly from a Greek verb meaning touch or titillate lasciviously, tickle.

-Wikipedia definition

When I was in the Air Force doing my payback time for them paying for med school, I had to be on call semi-regularly. There were about 8 doctors who took call for the non-pilots who used the Air Force clinic. We would alternate a week at a time carrying the on-call cell phone. As there was no full hospital on the base, the calls mostly consisted of telling patients whether they could go to the off-base local hospital ER or had to wait for the clinic hours in the morning.

The pilots and student pilots had their own 4 docs called *flight surgeons* (not that they actually were surgeons or did surgery, but it sounds cooler) who took care of & call for them. This had a very good reason besides the fact that, unsurprisingly, pilots are the prima donnas of the Air Force. They are very strictly regulated on what medicines they can take as it could potentially affect their ability to safely fly a plane if they took something that affected their alertness or judgment. Even something as simple as Benadryl could leave them feeling hung-over the next day and make them go crash, boom. And the Air Force takes it very seriously when they lose a multimillion-dollar plane and a pilot they have spent thousands of dollars training to fly said plane. I'd like to think they care about dead people too & I am sure they do, but as they are fond of saying: 'The needs (including financial needs) of the Air Force come first …'

I was in between the first Gulf War and 9-11. At that time all the services were in a weird kind of limbo. I noticed that the best way to get a promotion at that time was to be able to put in your *hopefully* promotion packet/semi-annual review the key phrase: 'Saved the Air Force X (the higher X the better) dollars by Y.' Y usually was some heroic act like outsourcing who the base bought toner from and saving $2 per cartridge. Not quite as sexy or cool as: 'Took out a nest of enemy snipers by eating their livers raw while being simultaneously fired at by 2000 enemy AK-47s and then carried out his entire platoon on his back at the same time while running through a lake of boiling acid.' Or some other actually heroic act.

Probably due to this overall un-coolness factor the Air Force was having trouble recruiting pilots. Many people with a college degree (even if it was in something not at all related to flying a plane, like art) who joined the Air Force for whatever reason besides wanting to become a pilot, were forced to become pilots. These hard pickings led to some not very happy people going to pilot training. My then future ex-wife was a therapist in the clinic and saw several of these poor guys. It also led to some not very sharp pilot trainees.

One day the on-call medical technician called me because they couldn't get ahold of the on-call flight surgeon & this guy wouldn't stop bothering them. He was one of the dull blades among the current group of pilot trainees. The tech asked me to take the call just to get the guy off their backs. My first response was 'You know I don't like pilots, but put him on the phone.'

The dull blade asked me 'I want to know how it would affect my flight status if I get tested for something.' I of course replied that I wouldn't know anything about flight status but asked what he wanted to be tested for. His answer was 'I think it's called **clitoris**.'

Of course, he meant **chlamydia**, one of the many venereal diseases you can get from unprotected sex. Easily prevented by using a condom but remember we are talking about the plastic knife that accidentally gets put in the cutlery drawer with the real ones.

The clitoris is quite a different matter entirely. **He** didn't have one. The clitoris as mentioned in the definition that starts this story is the female equivalent of the penis. Take an embryonic clit, add testosterone and it develops into a penis. Just like a penis it is incredibly sensitive and many (most?) women cannot achieve an orgasm without some form of clitoral stimulation. As young men tend to be pretty clueless & care only about themselves getting off anyway, many young women don't find sex to be nearly as rewarding as men, since men are practically guaranteed an orgasm every time without nearly as much special attention.

I had to immediately cover the mouthpiece of the phone to laugh uproariously before I tried to as neutrally and non-judgmentally as possible tell him that he was probably talking about chlamydia & that the clitoris was part of the female anatomy. Between every few words, I had to cover the mouthpiece so I didn't laugh in his ear …

The irony of the situation is that if he didn't even know what the clitoris was, much less that he should be doing something with it, the odds were probably relatively high he was smart enough to have had unprotected sex with some skank or even a ho at the local brothel just the other side of the border with Mexico and quite likely did pick up a little chlamydia as a parting gift.

DEAF DUMB AND BLIND

Jules: So, tell me again about the hash bars.

Vincent: Okay, what you wanna know?

Jules: Hash is legal there, right?

Vincent: Yeah, it's legal, but it ain't a hundred percent legal. I mean, you can't walk into a restaurant, roll a joint and start puffing away. You're only supposed to smoke in your home or certain designated places.

Jules: And those are hash bars?

Vincent: It breaks down like this: it's legal to buy it, it's legal to own it, and if you're the proprietor of a hash bar, it's legal to sell it. It's legal to carry it, but that doesn't really matter 'cause get a load of this, all right? If you get stopped by the cops in Amsterdam, it's illegal for them to search you. I mean, that's a right the cops in Amsterdam *don't* have.

Jules: *[laughing]* Oh, man! I'm going, that's all there is to it. I'm f**king going.

Vincent: Yeah baby, you'd dig it the most. But you know what the funniest thing about Europe is?

Jules: What?

Vincent: It's the little differences. I mean, they got the same shit over there that they got here, but it's just, it's just there it's a little different.

Jules: Example?

Vincent: All right. Well, you can walk into a movie theater in Amsterdam and buy a beer. And I don't mean just like in no paper cup, I'm talking about a glass of beer. And in Paris, you can buy a beer at McDonald's. And you know what they call a Quarter Pounder with Cheese in Paris?

Jules: They don't call it a Quarter Pounder with Cheese?

Vincent: Nah, man, they got the metric system. They wouldn't know what the f**k a Quarter Pounder is.

Jules: What do they call it?

Vincent: They call it a "Royale with Cheese."

Jules: "Royale with Cheese."

Vincent: That's right.

Jules: What do they call a Big Mac?

Vincent: A Big Mac's a Big Mac, but they call it *"Le Big Mac"*.

Jules: *"Le Big Mac."* [*laughs*] What do they call a Whopper?

Vincent: I dunno, I didn't go into Burger King. But, you know what they put on French fries in Holland instead of ketchup?

Jules: What?

Vincent: Mayonnaise.

Jules: God damn!

Vincent: I seen them do it, man, they f**king drown them in that shit.

Jules: That's some f**ked up shit.

-from the movie *Pulp Fiction*

My first real international trip was between med school & internship (trips across the border to Tijuana or Rocky Point/Puerto Penasco to get drunk & party don't really count). This was '95 not too long after *Pulp Fiction* came out. And of course, that was a huge extra reason to go. Not that I needed one. My whole life I have been a big reader. That has given me the desire to really see the places I've read about. And since so much of the English and American classics are from the deadly dull and constricted (at least on the surface) Victorian Era, I preferred the French and Russians. Lot more actually goin' on in their literature overall. Even before I read the book, I saw and fell in love with the old movie version of the Hunchback of Notre Dame. And of course, the book is better than the movie, as is almost always the case. It is a heartrendingly sad middle ages version of Forrest Gump (actually the other way around). But they didn't treat the mentally or physically disabled nor minorities nearly as well back then as they did in Forrest's time. The poor hunchback bell ringer at Notre Dame (one of the best and most impressive Gothic churches in Europe) was also developmentally disabled. The book starts at what to him is the best day of his life. They make him the official king of a local festival. He gets all kinds of attention and food and even gets to wear a crown. Fortunately for him he doesn't realize it is the Festival of Fools & he is the King of Fools. It goes downhill from there. He falls for another outcast, the local beautiful Gypsy girl. Of course, she doesn't even realize it nor would settle for him anyway. When she gets in trouble, he saves her by taking her into the church & shouting from the balcony 'Sanctuary! Sanctuary!' And it has to end badly. It became my favorite book for years.

I ended up going from Madrid by train to Rome then Paris and Amsterdam. I couldn't really afford it and ended up maxing out my credit cards even with staying in cheap tourist hotels called pensions or in youth hostels. When I got to Amsterdam and tried to check into the youth hostel I was going to say at, I found out my card didn't work there. This was back way before the internet and at the time, there were 2 systems used for credit cards or ATMs. And not every place was set up to use both. This was on the first of 2 or 3 days there. And I had no cash. Fortunately, the guy at the desk in the hostel told me that there was 1 ATM in all of Amsterdam that accepted cards that used my system. Otherwise I would have been begging and sleeping on the street or making a collect call home asking for my parents to send money by Western Union or whatever.

But it was still one of the best and most impactful times of my life. I saw all the big museums and architectural sites everywhere I went. I practiced all the local languages. I spent Bastille Day (the French version of July 4th) at a city-wide street party in Paris and caught an outdoor James Brown concert. I met a girl on the train to Rome and we ended up staying in the same pension there and saw the city together. I used my newly minted medical degree to check out a guy who had a minor accident on his scooter outside the Vatican when I was with her. I got to see some beautiful women both locals and tourists and flirted with a few. I ate foods I never would have known about otherwise and saw how the 'Italian food' we have here isn't really much like the real thing. I got to re-read *Hunchback* on the plaza in front of Notre Dame & even had someone take a picture of me using my backpack as a hump and shouting 'Sanctuary!' My hostel in Amsterdam even had a hash bar built into it. But of course, I would never have even entered such a den of iniquity ...

More importantly it opened my eyes to so much of the world and how differently things work outside the US. And I was not your average clueless American. I was highly educated and I had read quite a bit of European literature by then. I spoke passable Spanish and brought my books for that, Italian, Dutch and French (but hadn't really had time to do more than a brief look at them yet). I had guide books for all the places I was going. And had actually read them & pre-planned out where I wanted to go. But ...

Those little differences still tripped me up. And the preconceptions of Americans overseas by the natives were a big thing too. Since before the US was a country, the British have been taking 'the Grand Tour' of continental Europe after formal schooling as a kind of finishing school for life. In the 1800s, as the US got more prosperous, Americans got into the mix. It became such a big thing that Mark Twain wrote several nonfiction travel books about his own trips abroad, starting with *Innocents Abroad*. He satirized his clueless fellow passengers taking a Grand Tour of Europe and the Holy Land. It is still funny and true to life today. Beginning with the nationalistic, incurious, superior Brits and continuing to the even more so Americans; English speaking tourists have gotten a bad reputation in Europe. This is worst in France. Some of it is sour grapes. The French used to have the predominant **CULTURE** in the world. Now, American trash 'culture' is more popular. But we tend to be incurious, nationalistic and superior, dress like we are going to the beach or mall no matter where we are going and usually don't even try to use the local language. Can't see why that would make us unpopular.

It started as I was boarding the plane to Spain. A cute Spanish girl saw my Spanish book and said 'too late for that now'. Spain has some of the best food in the world. The now worldwide obsession with being a foodie and eating molecular cuisine (lots of foams and meringues made from unusual things, food that has been destroyed and put back together again in a different form, 'sous vide' cooking in a sealed plastic bag and a hot water bath) all started in a corner of Spain. Even the traditional cooking of Spain has a distinctive character formed from its mix of European and North African roots as a former colony of Morocco. I had no clue (and no $). My most memorable meal in Madrid was a dry ham sandwich. Spanish ham can be the most expensive and arguably best in the world at the higher levels. I wasn't buying from those kinds of places and didn't enjoy or appreciate what I was eating at all.

My time in Rome was mostly spent in a bubble with a new girl so no glaring issues arose. It was pretty weird for me to be staying in a tourist hotel with no bathroom in the room, just one per floor shared by everyone there. And there is an old joke in Europe that I'm sure is a little less true anymore: in Spain they speak pretty good English, in France they speak really good English, in Italy they speak really good Italian. True.

On the train to Paris things took a turn for the worse. My car mate on the train was French from a small town in the North. When I got in for our 6ish hour ride I asked if he spoke English. Him said no. Since we were going to France, I started reviewing French. I asked him and he DID speak Spanish. I started out asking him in Spanish the French words for common things like Where, How Much, etc. Before long, he looked at me and asked 'Are you American?' when I said yes & he realized that I wasn't one of THOSE Americans, he became fluent in English in about 10 seconds. He saw I was reading a book by a classical French writer and told me how the same guy had written a book about his hometown. He gave me his # and told me that I could stay at his place if I ever went there. He told me his life story and didn't stop talking until we got to Paris.

In the capital of French **CULTURE**, the French get even snobbier and nastier. And my own cluelessness didn't help. I was trying to economize on food so I ordered lait chaud, hot milk, in a cafe. But I was thinking the chaud meant cold. You know, cXXd, related languages, etc. Not quite, nor very good. And when I went to the counter to ask for a hard-boiled egg instead of waiting for the waiter to come to me, I got the fisheye from the waiter and other locals. I saw the Napoleonic tower of the Vendome in the distance and asked some local girls in horrible French what it was, more fisheye.

And those are just a few examples. Even more glaring was just the difference in clothing. The typical American travel outfit of baseball hat, T-shirt, shorts or jeans (or OMG sweat pants!) and white tennis shoes make an American standout from miles away. The Europeans may wear (nice) jeans but typically wear real adult shirts and shoes even to go to the corner store. And dress even better to go to dinner or a concert.

From the time I got back to this day, I haven't worn and now don't even own jeans or tennis shoes. I may wear sweat pants or shorts as weather permits if I am doing simple errands on a day off, but if I am going out to dinner or anyplace nice, I dress like an adult. Surprisingly (?) enough, people semi-regularly ask if I am from Europe or elsewhere when I am out and about at home ... Kind of a sad statement about American 'culture', no?

DOIN' THE BUTT

She was doin' the butt, hey pretty, pretty
When you get that notion
Put your backfield in motion, hey
Doin' the butt, hey sexy, sexy
Ain't nothing wrong
If you wanna do the butt, all night long

-from the song *Da Butt* by EU

Everyone who works in an ER has a story or two about what patients have put up their butts'. In school I read a book by a famous coroner during a ski trip that included a story about a guy (it's almost *always* a guy) who switched out the seat on his stationary bike with a broom handle and would pedal vigorously while riding the broom handle. Unfortunately for him (& later his family when they found him) he slipped and perforated his colon and died there. Nice.

There used to be a webpage in the early days of the internet called The Butt Page. It was full of stories, pictures and x-rays submitted by various medical staff about things people put up their butts'. I am sure it was pulled down as a consequence of patient privacy laws since then. One old WW II vet was using an artillery shell to push his protruding hemorrhoids back in for years until it slipped. I don't recommend doing that at home ...

One of my most memorable ones was a guy who came in holding a jacket or some such over his backside. His story was that he had passed out drunk the nite before and his 'friends' had played a cruel joke on him. 'They' had shoved the handle of a portable umbrella up his ass when was unconscious. It certainly wasn't him. He's not gay or anything like that. Pretty sure that's not the way it happened. Can't picture any straight guys wanting to be that closely associated with their friend's ass.

It had got stuck. Once you get something past a certain point a vacuum effect happens that sucks whatever you put up there in and it can be near impossible to get out without surgery. He broke off the umbrella at the metal pole and came on in.

The surgeons put him up in the stirrups like a woman delivering a baby, put forceps on either side of it and pulled it out. Blood was gushing out of his rectum during and after. I'm sure this was not the right way to go about it. They should have taken him right to the operating room and opened him up to get it out safely. Hopefully they didn't tear or otherwise pop his anus and or colon. Either way, he went upstairs after and was their problem for then on.

Another guy had one of those huge black metal cop flashlights (AKA mag lites) up there. A good 2 feet were sticking out of him. Pretty impressive and frightening sight. This guy went right up to the OR fortunately.

The only woman I've ever seen who was doin' the butt was actually a false alarm. She was a big-time crack head who would come in regularly because she was delirious from the crack. The last time I saw her, she came in saying she had a 12-inch-long black dildo up her ass. There was no such thing on the rectal exam as far as my fingers would go. And I have pretty long fingers. Nor anything on the X-ray. The only thing in her ass and every other cell in her body, was so much crack that she was crazy as shit (appropriately enough).

My most memorable butt player was another false alarm. This time for financial gain. This clown came in about 3 in the morning saying the cops butt raped him with their hands when they arrested him earlier that night. He was all agitated and didn't seem quite right in the head. He insisted I exam him down there so he could go after the cops later.

In cases of reported rape or similar assaults specially trained nurses called Sexual Assault Nurse Examiners (SANE) see the patients at special centers after you call the police to take them there. The SANE name is usually a misnomer as most of the nurses who choose to do this disheartening job are not exactly sane. They are needed however as it is very complicated and requires a special kit to get the various evidence needed and properly document the exam to confirm or refute the charges. Or to come up with an innocent diagnosis like a child with pinworms at their rectum causing them to itch down there, not having been assaulted by Uncle Bob. Also, this saves the ER staff from being forced to testify in a trial. Although sexual assaults on men are much rarer, they are trained to take care of them as well.

If I had been thinking it through, I would have called the police to take him away. Stupid me, I did a rectal exam and documented no trauma but that he did have a trace of blood in his poop on the test. Of course, this could come from anything between either end from bleeding gums to an ulcer. Then I kicked him out of my ER.

I heard about him next when some ambulance chasing hack attorney sent me a subpoena to testify in his case against the police. The ambulance chaser didn't answer the phone when I called him back. I left a message saying he had no case as there was no chain of custody on his client's ass between the police station and the ER. And that he could have had blood in his poop from anything from an ulcer to rough anal sex or putting a rutabaga up his ass for sexual pleasure. I told him that if he didn't cancel the subpoena, he would lose his case as I would testify the same.

Then I called the attorney for the police. She told me this guy was already in jail for gang activity when he brought the lawsuit. And bipolar. And he had told me when he was in the ER that he smoked pot. Whatever your feelings about pot, it is always a bad idea for schizophrenics or bipolars as it weakens their already loose grip on reality. She also told me that the cops don't even have gloves in their cars, so of course they were never going to butt rape someone with their hands. And the entire time he was in jail, this goofball was in camera screaming that he had to go so he wanted the cops to search his butt for drugs and let him go. As he was doing this, he was spreading his butt cheeks.

The ambulance chaser wouldn't drop the case, so I finally had to go to court. As he called me in to the courtroom to testify, I told him 'You are a real piece of work'. When it was my turn to testify, I said while looking Goofy straight in the eyes that the blood in his poop could have come from anything including rough anal sex or shoving something up there for sexual pleasure. This big, muscular gangbanger's face fell and he put his head down on the table when I said this. Then the ambulance chaser confronted me about what I said on his answering machine. I said 'Yes, I did say that because he had no case and it was true'. Needless to say, he lost the case. I left a message on the ambulance chaser's machine saying 'HAH!' when I got home.

DONALD TRUMP MADE ME SMOKE CRACK

Last call for alcohol
Last call for your freedom of speech
Drink up. Happy hour is now enforced by law
Don't forget our house special, it's called a Trickie
Dickie Screwdriver
It's got one-part Jack Daniels, two parts purple
Kool-Aid,
and a jigger of formaldehyde
from the jar with Hitler's brain in it we got in the back
storeroom
I am The Donald
Real man with fascist cravings
Still you made me president
Human rights will soon go 'way
I will be Führer one day
I will command all of you
Your kids will pray in school
But only if they're Christian, fool
Oklahoma Über Alles
Über Alles Oklahoma

Ku Klux Klan will control you
Still you think it's natural
Border watchin' for the master race
And always wear the happy face

Close your eyes, can't happen here
Big Bro' on white horse is near
The Nazis won't come back, you say
Join the army or you will pay
Oklahoma Über Alles
Über Alles Oklahoma
Yeah, that's it. Just relax
Have another drink, few more pretzels, little
more MSG
Turn on those Dallas Cowboys on your TV
Lock your doors. Close your mind
It's time for the two-minute warning

Now it is nineteen eighty-four
Are you ready for the third world war?!?
Knock-knock at your front door
It's the Make America Great Again capped secret
police
They'll draft you and deport your dark-skinned niece

You'll go quietly to boot camp
They'll shoot you dead, make you a man
Don't you worry, it's for a cause
Feeding global corporations' claws
Die on our best ever poison gas
Iraq or Afghanistan
You will choke you little chump, when you mess with
President Trump
Making money for President Trump
And all the friends of President Trump

Oklahoma Über Alles
Über Alles Oklahoma …

-my original song

During the 1980 elections, when then (& now) California governor Jerry Brown was still in the game, lots of people on the Right were afraid of what would happen if this crazy hippie won the presidency. After all, Jerry was way ahead of his time and pretty hard to the Left. He was talking about meditation (which is now nearly mainstream) being taught in schools, (voluntary) sterilization as a form of birth & population control, and dating Linda Ronstadt the rock singer. To make fun of this hysteria the hyper-liberal, hyper-sarcastic punk band the Dead Kennedys wrote a song called *California Uber Alles* (California Over All) about the hippie fascist state which Brown would bring on once he got into power. The title comes from the theme song of Nazi Germany, *Deutschland Uber Alles* (Germany O.A.). When Reagan won, they tweaked the lyrics into a follow up called *We've Gotta Bigger Problem Now.* Now that we are in the age of the great orange Beast, I rejiggered the lyrics again to account for the new reality. I call my version *Oklahoma Uber Alles.*

A few months after the election I saw a 45-year-old patient who smoked like crazy and had just fallen off the wagon into a crack pipe. He was there for chest pain and between the crack, the Marlboro, and the fact that his dad died of a heart attack at 40; he needed to stay to make sure he didn't have a heart attack coming on. He got all the standard tests in the ER and all the standard medicines. He was kind of a touchy, irritable guy (surprise, surprise I'm sure considering he was coming off crack). I asked him when was the last time he went to AA. His answer was that he had been going regular and had been sober (but not for the Marlboro, of course) for 18 months.

Cigarettes are nearly always the first drug used by alcoholics and drug addicts. 90% of them smoke. And if you smoke it is 90% likely that you drink at least a little. Partly addictive personality &/ or genes, partly just that the incredibly poor judgement and desire for a short-term stupid high that was bad enough for you to think smoking was a good idea didn't stop with that 1st bad decision. It is also the last drug given up by most alcoholics and addicts, if ever. AA justifies not even trying to quit until you have been sober from your other drug or drugs a year. This is despite evidence showing that if you continue to smoke, you are more likely to relapse on your other drugs. This makes perfect sense. How can you continue to get high on nicotine multiple times a day while trying to convince yourself that getting high is a bad idea? I think the AA position on this is slanted because Bill W., one of the 2 founders of AA, died of emphysema after continuing to smoke the rest of his otherwise sober life.

Then came the election, which threw him for a loop, as it did most people with teeth. He got depressed and felt hopeless and ended up getting back on the crack. We commiserated about the Trump-ness. And as I noticed he was pretty heavily tatted up, I asked him if he was into punk back in the day, particularly the Dead Kennedys. He was a big fan, so I printed up the song above for him. He liked it a lot. I talked to him about how he couldn't let that guy give him a heart attack. And about how that was still just an excuse. **He** was the one who stopped going to AA and started going to the dealer instead. And about how he needed to get back into AA or else.

Then I told him how I had the whole Trump mess taken care of. I asked him if he remembered the movie *Taxi Driver*. I reminded him of how De Niro played a schizophrenic who had a crush on Jodie Foster and tried to impress her by killing the presidential candidate. And I asked if he remembered John Hinckley, Jr. Hinckley is a real schizophrenic. He **really** liked the movie *Taxi Driver*. He also **really** liked Jodie Foster. He **really** shot Reagan in '83 to impress her. He just got released from the boobie hatch the summer before the election. Then I told him how right before I went into work that nite, I sent a letter to Hinckley saying: 'Hey John, I just saw Trump on youtube grabbing Jodie Foster's p***y'. He went upstairs with a smile on his face …

I saw him a few months later as he came back in for chest pain. He was still smoking the Marlboro and the crackboro. He needed to stay again of course. He also wanted to go outside to smoke (like I mentioned above, that bad judgement doesn't stop with your 1st cigarette). He was being seen by the swing shift doctor. Those two didn't get along at all. Granted the guy is an irritable crackhead, but then my colleague tends to make **me** look like Mr. Congeniality. Not a small feat. I love the guy and just return his sarcasm straight back at him. Lots of others not so much. He is an acquired taste. If you take him for what he is and don't take him personally, he can be a real cool guy. Our patient wasn't in a forgiving mood. He ended up leaving Against Medical Advice. I even tried to calm him down and get him to stay but he wasn't in the mood and left.

Fortunately, he came back a few hours later and by this time, my colleague had gone home. And he had mellowed enough that he was willing to stay. Fortunately, the bonding we had done earlier was still there. I arranged for him to get upstairs quick since all the tests had been done the first time that nite, so he didn't have a chance to act up and storm out again.

DON'T CARJACK A GUY WITH A SAWED OFF

Just Say No to drugs and violence.

-ludicrously ineffective '80s commercial

I went to a medical school which is based at the county hospital near downtown LA. It is also near skid row, the massive homeless encampment in downtown. And in East LA which has lots of largely Latino gangs. And what used to be called South Central LA, which is home to many black and Latino gangs. Used to be, because South Central had such a bad rep & was name checked in so many gangster rap songs that they officially changed the name to 'South LA'. Great example of bullshit re-branding rather than fix the myriad problems like drugs, crime, poverty, prostitution, bad schools, etc. And the day after the name change, all the drugs and crime went away to be replaced by affluent white Yuppies ... Yeah, right.

Regardless, there was a lot of gang and other violence so it was a great place to learn, but not so much to live in.

One day while I was rotating on trauma surgery, this guy came in had who tried to carjack somebody. He was a huge muscular thug, but unfortunately for him the guy he held up had a sawed-off shotgun. And was faster.

By the time he got to us, he had 1 blast thru the bottom/back angle of his jaw and out the other side. There was room to put several fingers straight thru from one side of his face to the other. And in one shoulder. And in one ass cheek. The Ear Nose Throat guys had to put some kind of plastic or metal plates in each side of his jaw to replace the missing bone & wired his jaw shut for at least a month to heal. And put a tracheostomy in his low neck so he could still breathe with all the swelling and bleeding in his airway. We cleaned out the fist size holes in his shoulder and ass. If he hadn't been so muscular, they would have likely ended up much deeper and messed up some important stuff. Because he was so jacked, they didn't go into anything that mattered. I actually pulled the shot gun wadding (cartridge) out of the hole in his shoulder.

Needless to say, he stayed for over a month recovering. And since he couldn't talk with the trach, he had a pad of paper he used to ask & answer questions, etc. Not surprisingly given his occupation of carjacker & the bad schools in the area, he wasn't much of a scholar. His writing, vocabulary etc. were like a not very bright 2nd grader.

Eventually he got some kind of infection & got a little delirious. When I was doing my rounds on the guy while he was out of his head, he motioned to the paper because he wanted to tell me something. When he was done, I read the message. It said: 'I want your ass'. Nice.

I think it meant he (a black thuggish guy) wanted to beat me (a skinny white guy) up. Maybe he was an Undercover Brother (look it up on urbandictionary.com) and wanted to do other things to my ass and was acting without a filter because he was delirious. I'll never know.

A month or so later I saw him walking the halls going to X-Ray or something like that. This big buff guy was skinnier than me by then after having his jaw wired shut, the sick, no gym time …

Hopefully he learned from this mistake & is on the straight & narrow now.

DON'T TRY THIS AT HOME

Don't try this at home.

-Legal disclaimer shown right before someone does something really stupid on TV.

'Frida' was a heroin addict. When you have been using heroin for a while, all your accessible veins get scarred up & it is almost impossible to get a needle into a vein anywhere. Not very good if you gotta go to the hospital & get an IV. Nurses will tell heroin addicts: 'Show me your good vein if you want the pain medicine.' I tell the male addicts: 'Well, we can always put it in the vein on the top of your penis …' Never had to follow through on that idle threat yet. After there are no veins left and since they still make heroin, you must find some way of getting it in you.

Some people will bear down to make the neck veins stand out & shoot up in their neck. Nice. And pretty easy to break the tip off the needle inside the veins since you are doing this blind by feel or maybe with a mirror. People have been known to have a half dozen needles broke off in their necks. The commoner fix (pun intended) is called **skin popping**. Not nearly as fun as it doesn't get the heroin to your brain in one big rush like when it gets into a vein. It has to leach out slowly from some random place under the skin. And you end up being covered with little abscesses that eventually turn into little knotty scars on your entire body. Sexy. Which should be a serious damper on selling your body, which is the easiest way to get $ for heroin. Your average toothless, smelly, crazy heroin addict is pretty nice looking without skin popping scars all over. But then some people will hit anything with a hole in it. As they say: 'Every pot has a lid.' And my version: 'And so does every garbage can.'

Frida got admitted for something on my service when I was doing Internal Medicine. When you are the student on an inpatient service like that at a county hospital **you** are the one going from bed to bed on your patients at 6 in the morning before rounds to draw blood before the team makes its way around the entire service later in the morning. This, while a real pain in the ass, is the best way to learn. My colleagues who went to med schools attached to nice private hospitals didn't get to see or do nearly as much as I did.

Since Frida had no veins to speak of, I went for the easy way. I stuck the needle straight into the femoral vein in the groin which is about as big around as a pencil so it's a much bigger target. It **is** trickier to get to though. You can't use a tourniquet for starters. Nor see or feel it. You have to find the pulse from the femoral artery next door and go blindly. If you miss you could easily get it into the artery by mistake. This can cause it to get infected, bleed or if you were to accidentally inject something (especially something dirty like heroin) there, you might even lose the leg.

As I was getting the blood out so apparently easily with good flow, I looked up at Frida's face. Her eyes were about as big as ping pong balls and she was salivating all over the bed. I made sure to tell her: 'DON'T TRY THIS AT HOME!' unless she wanted to lose her leg.

A few weeks later she came back with the paramedics to the ER when I was on there. The medic started telling her story: 'This is Melba Jones a xx-year-old with a history of …' I cut him off and told everyone: 'This is Frida Smith, she has HIV. Still using the heroin Frida?'

ECO-HOSTEL

Hostel: Movie. The film tells the story of two college students traveling across Europe, who find themselves preyed upon by a mysterious group that tortures and kills kidnapped back-packers.

-Wikipedia definition

When we went to Peru, we did a lot more than the average visitor. We flew in to the capitol, Lima. It is a charming coastal city but doesn't seem to have been very memorable. I can't really remember anything about it. Cusco, on the other hand was much more interesting. It is several thousand feet high for starters. It was the capitol of the Incan empire and later the de facto Spanish capitol of south America. It still has a very native feel. The people on average look more native than Spanish, unlike most of South America. It seems like the Spanish, intentionally or not, took care of the native population more 'successfully' in South than North America. Peru, maybe because of the forbidding altitude and difficulty reaching the altiplano (high plateau) kept much more of a native feel & look than in most of Spanish Latin America.

One of the big holdovers from native times is the local delicacy, **cuy** (coo-ee). Also known as guinea pig. I of course had to try it. Apparently, they cook them whole, fur and all. The hair burns off & the tendons shrink as they cook. This makes them come to the table with the arms & legs retracted, but more strikingly the jaw froze wide open like it's pissed off & going to bite you. Nice. I bought a T-shirt there that has a cuy on a plate with fries & the question: 'Do you want fries with that guinea pig?' much later we visited a church on the altiplano near Lake Titicaca. Admit it, you just had a little inner chuckle about the name Titty Caca ... Just like the Catholic church turned Roman, Celtic & German holidays into Christmas, Easter and All Soul's Day to attract people (and their $), they did something similar there. At the painting of the Last Supper on the church wall, I found out that cuy was served at the dinner. 'This wine is my blood, this bread is my flesh, this cuy is the bacteria in my colon ...'

They also built churches on top of native temples all over the world. Keeps the people (and their $) coming to the same place every Sunday. The old Temple of the Sun there got a Catholic church built on top of it. Apparently, my idea about the Last Supper is right & God IS an ancient Incan. They had a big earthquake there years ago. The Catholic add-on (built by modern civilized Europeans, not some ignorant savages in loincloths) largely collapsed. The original Incan work is still going strong. You cannot slip a thin knife blade between 2 bricks (hundreds of years older & made without mortar no less)!

Machu Pichu is awe inspiring of course. A lost city built on one side of a big green mountain valley out of massive white blocks. Even more inspiring when you realize the rocks were hand carried from the far side of the valley. While the Incans domesticated llamas (like a smaller, hairier, cuter camel), they were too small or maybe they just never thought of using them as beasts of burden. Again, no mortar, no can stick a blade between 2 blocks.

After seeing the sites in Lima & the altiplano, we went off the map to the Peruvian Amazon. This is getting to be a more popular option for trekkers to Peru. Since we prefer to go to more offbeat places and avoid the crowds when we can, we chose the lesser visited, more pristine Amazon location. Since Lorena works in global warming & sustainability and it is just a nice idea, we picked a place that my guidebook recommended as an Ecolodge. This implies a smaller carbon footprint, less pollution, etc.

We flew into the small city nearby late in the afternoon. The sun was going down by the time we got to the lagoon and the boat that was going to take us to the lodge. We then rode the boat 20 or 30 minutes in the dark. As we were getting deeper into the jungle, Lorena was gradually getting more nervous. 'They could just kidnap us here & nobody would ever find us.' I told her 'Of course not, relax.'

When we finally got close the boatman shouted to the shore & a generator started up and lights came on in the small lodge. They showed us to our hut. Literally a straw hut. And not in very good repair. More little holes than you could count between the reeds or whatever made it up. A hole in the ceiling of the bathroom bigger than your head opening up into the straw roof. They turned the lights off after an hour or so. I tried to use my reading glasses with a little light built into each earpiece. Within seconds hundreds of small insects surrounded my head drawn to the lights. Within seconds the lights got turned off. Then it started to rain hard all nite long.

Since it was not very comfortable and only about 9:30, we couldn't sleep. Lorena asked me to tell her something to kill time. Recently I had gotten into a discussion about movies with a nurse at work. She is one different girl. Multiple piercings & tats, vegan, hates (most) people but spends her free nites capturing feral cats & getting them fixed or into homes. Very cool person & a good nurse, a true original. Her favorite movies are horror flicks. But not just your average horror. She is a fan of slasher films. And even worse the ones called torture porn, like the *Saw* movies. Her favorite is *Hostel*. As in youth hostel, the cheap dorm like hotels for young people. The hostel in the movie however is a front for guys who sell the 'guests' to depraved people who want to hunt the greatest game, MAN. Horrid concept. Horrid sounding movie. I was reminded of it by Lorena's boating paranoia & it kept rolling around in my head as it is just so mind-boggling that people would actually enjoy a movie like that. Much less that it could be this girl's favorite. I made the mistake of sharing this with Lorena. Big mistake. I don't think Lorena sleep much that nite at all.

By the morning we were still alive and not dumped in the swamp somewhere. I consider that a win. We were woken up that & every morning by the chickens & roosters outside of our holey hut. Nice. Lorena went to the toilet seat-less bathroom and came running out screaming. There was a cute little frog hopping in the shower. She didn't see him as cute. Later we went to the saddest zoo in the world. The caged spider monkey was super cute and wouldn't let go of my hand as he looked deep into my eyes asking me to kill him or set him free. A howler monkey was tied to a pole by a chain around his neck. He jumped onto my head and shoulders and didn't want to let go either. When we got back, there was a spider with a leg span at least as big as my hand on the inside of the window. He was pretty easy to kill. The cricket the next morning, not so much. Amazon crickets have wings and can fly. When I tried to step on it, it started flying around the room and landed on Lorena's ankle. She **loved** that.

That day we went fishing for piranha & actually caught one or two. The look like small perch or sunfish with big teeth. It would take hundreds to actually eat you.

We went from there to the airport glad to be going back to civilization.

Don't ever suggest to Lorena that we stay in an Ecolodge ...

FRANKENSTEIN

Prometheus was one of the titans, the earlier, weaker gods of the Greeks. He saw humanity struggling before the discovery of fire, so he decided to be the first humanitarian. He took some fire from the gods and showed the humans how to use it.

The gods weren't happy since now people were less under their thumbs. They took Prometheus and chained him to a rock. Every day an eagle came and ripped out his liver then ate it. Every night it grew back. He only stayed there for a few eons until Hercules unchained him as he was passing through.

-the myth of Prometheus and the gift of fire

The book *Frankenstein* is subtitled 'A modern Prometheus'. And if you've never read the actual book, it is quite different from the movies. No 'Bread good. Fire bad.' The monster is very smart and reads books by Plato and Milton. He tries to get Dr. Frankenstein to make him a female companion, then he treats the doc like the gods treated Prometheus when he refuses.

Doc Frankenstein becomes obsessed with what separates living from dead tissue and how it might be possible to bring something back to life.

I got *Frankenstein* when I was 10 for Christmas. The whole idea of what makes someone alive and Dr. Frankenstein's quest to understand how to give it back to dead tissue made me curious about what being alive means and how the brain allows us to think. This curiosity has stayed with me to this day.

I can remember having to do a report on the brain about the same time for school. It was pretty crude. 'This part allows us to do this function.' Since then I have taken all kinds of classes on psychology, neuroanatomy and physiology. I have read several books on how the brain works by some of the top neuroscientists around. And the state of the art in a very real way hasn't got very far from 'This part allows us to do this function.' They can sort of sketch out how a very basic memory is formed. And have explained a few big picture things as well as added functions to parts, but they haven't even started to be able to describe a thought.

I can directly link reading *Frankenstein* to my eventually becoming a doctor. The quest of Dr. Frankenstein has infected me as well. But I don't have any plans to re-animate corpses. For now …

I BEEN WORKIN ON
THE RAILROAD

I love you, you love me, we're a happy family.

-song guaranteed to make any adult want to commit
Barneycide from the kids' show *Barney & Friends*

Nursing homes are overall, horrible hopeless places full of adults in a death spiral often with their patient/family wishes form filled out with Full Code. At least partially because the doctors can't bill for seeing a patient after they die, nor can families get that social security check. This means if your heart or breathing stops they will call 911 & do everything to save your life. This can include breaking ribs during CPR, shocking you and shoving a big plastic tube down your throat into your lungs so a machine can breathe for you. Even more fun than it sounds. And of course, people in nursing homes don't have much or any active, enjoyable life left to save. Or often even a brain left to know if they are. Usually there is enough left to feel all that discomfort. And the same Full Code, hopeless often brainless people are usually going to have their family sign them up for a feeding tube to be cut through the wall of their belly and dialysis if their kidneys go out. It's OK though, all this is paid out of **your** taxes. Nice. One old book about modern medicine calls demented nursing home patients GOMERs: Get Out of My Emergency Room. And notes that every gomer has their call (repetitive thing they say). As well as two rules of the hospital related to them: Gomers never die & Gomers go to ground (tend to fall-especially thanks to the stuff I talk about next paragraph). Not nice, but understandable and way too true.

And the staff at nursing homes tend to be the bottom feeders of the health care world. Either new grads who escape as soon as they can or the people without the skills or ambition to escape. They will send patients to the ER (usually inappropriately with basic EMTs instead of paramedics no matter how sick they are) so they can watch more TV. And of course, they lie to make this do-able. Short of breath with no oxygen in the blood becomes 'congestion' with normal blood oxygen once they are put on maximum oxygen. When they call to dump patients, if it is inappropriate, I get their name & tell them if you send the patient without paramedics and calling 911, I will be calling your boss in the am. Usually works. Many of the local docs will collude with them by telling them to send them to the far hospital where they work, rather than calling 911 and going to the closer hospital where they don't. You can't bill for taking care of a patient if they don't go to your hospital & get seen by you. Nice again. I tell the EMTs who get conned by these clowns that until proven otherwise, you cannot work at a nursing home unless you are lazy, stupid or incompetent. And the only way to get the sign on bonus is to be all 3. Sadly, all too true.

Anyway, now that that rant is over. I got a nursing home dump one night that was actually appropriate. It also ended up being one the weirdest patient scenes I have ever seen. And if you've read any of my other stories, you know that's saying something.

This lady had had a bad stroke that left one side of her body paralyzed and she was severely brain damaged. She had one hand in a special medical padded mitten because she would try to hit people with her good hand. And the fine, fine nursing home staff apparently dumped her in front of the TV with random shows on all day so they didn't have to deal with her. Consequently, she would repeatedly sing the Barney song that starts this story. Her other 'call' was to sing the title line of the 1800s song 'I been workin' on the railroad. She alternated between the 2 randomly.

Since she had an infection, we needed to do all kind of tests to find out what and where. Since women, in particular (guys got at least an extra 2 inches between the poo hole and the pee hole), especially demented or incontinent ones who use a diaper are more likely to get urine infections; we had to get urine. And since she wasn't gonna walk to the bathroom to pee in a cup, this meant we had to put a tube in her pee hole to get it out. Remember the padded mitten thing? Imagine how fun it was trying to do that as she was kicking and hitting.

We had to have one person hold her good arm and one each spread and hold a leg while someone else put in the tube. Somehow, I got to be the tube person, either because the nurses couldn't find the hole or just that there weren't enough hands.

As we got her held down and I was trying to put in the tube, she stated peeing by herself all over my (gloved) hand and singing 'I been working on the railroad' in a surprisingly powerful good voice.

Can you top that for weird as shit (weird as piss)?

INDIAN FOOD FOR THE BODY (AND SOUL?)

The 10 headed demon Ravana meditated for a thousand years, so the god Brahma gave him a wish. He wanted to be unable to be killed by any of the gods & Brahma said yes. Then he went on a killing spree and took over the world. Oops.

As part of his plan of world domination he went to the house of Shiva, the god of destruction (of the bad guys), yoga and meditation. He got all uppity with Shiva, who is supposedly the most powerful of the gods. Shiva responded by stepping on him. He couldn't kill him, but could have kept him from making any trouble for eternity.

Then Ravana started to sing a very nice pretty song. Shiva liked it. Since even this horrible demon could produce something so beautiful & since Shiva knew Ravana had things he was supposed to do in the world which would eventually work out for the greater good, Shiva let him go.

Since Ravana was still an evil demon, he continued to cause trouble until some of the gods arranged to be born as humans to kill him. But that is a totally different story …

-My version of part of the Indian epic story *Ramayana*

When I first read this story, it blew my mind. I like reading mythology, even the Judeo-Christian-Muslim ones, because the stories are engaging, they usually have some moral or symbolic point to make & they are a great lens on the society they came from. I had NEVER seen anything like this before anywhere else. The Greeks, Norse & especially desert monotheistic religions are all about an eye for an eye. Giant steals the apples of immortality; god X kills him. 'To the unbelievers: the fiery pit being tortured for eternity'. Even the first hippie, Jesus, said 'No one gets to The Father except through me. I am the Way & the Door.' Despite all that peace & love stuff, that means a lot of people going straight to Hell. Last I checked, there are 144 thousand vacancies in heaven. For the entire existence of humanity. There are over 144 thousand people in my city who think they got a reservation for the Hotel Heaven who are gonna be mighty disappointed if that's true. Since I'm a pure atheist, I'm ok with that. Light's out party's over.

India is different. They have a lot more acceptance for the bad stuff in life. Some of that might be that they have more poverty etc. than some places, but I am sure some of it comes from their religion & its different take on life. The dominant Indian culture, language and mythology is still part of the Indo-European family. This is why some of the basic rules and words of the languages from England to India are similar. English **video** is from the same root as Hindi **vidya** with similar meanings. Similarly, much of the Indian mythology is similar. There are gods that are analogous to Thor or Apollo (who are analogous to each other) for example.

Shiva is the wild card. Idols of Shiva have been found in South India that predate the invasion of white Aryans from the North. Shiva is an odd dude by Western standards. He is called the corpse god because he hangs out in cemeteries as a reminder of everyone's (even his) final address. He is the god of meditation and yoga. And he spends the greater part of his time meditating.

This profound shift in the religion away from the rest of the Western attitude to life has made India quite different as well. Even in the midst of some of the worst poverty around, the people are for the most part happy & less materialistic. The Buddha himself started out as a Hindu before his 'awakening' (the literal meaning of Buddha is awakened one). The modern Hindus have made him one of the 11 mortal incarnations (avatars) of the other big Indian god, Vishnu. Very little of the nuts and bolts of Buddhist philosophy is that far from Hinduism.

Meditation therefore is South India's gift to the world. And may explain some of the greater than might be expected happiness in India. The Hindus and Buddhists can tell you how in their theology, if you do enough meditation, you will get a better setup in the next life or maybe even get released from the cycle of rebirth and become a Buddha yourself. Not to mention all kinds of magical powers from prolonged meditation and yoga. The Buddhists have a type of meditation called walking meditation. You walk as mindfully as possible, trying to put all your attention into each footstep. Been there, tried that, bores me to tears. Maybe I'm just a shallow person and can't see the depths of awakening that can arise from something like that, blah, blah, blah …

Yoga, however, is something I do like and have done for over ten years, now practically daily, at least for 10 or 15 minutes. Back to walking meditation, if enlightenment and practice at paying attention to the NOW can be got from something as simple as mindful walking, imagine how much more useful as a form of meditation yoga can be. If you are holding a complicated yoga pose while trying to experience all the sensations it brings up in your body and trying to hold your entire body in the right position (at an increasing level of detail and complexity the further you go into yoga) and sweating etc., the last thing on your mind is your taxes. And then the class ends in at least a few minutes of more traditional still meditation where you just focus on your breathing and how you feel after the physical part of the class. The first yoga textbook barely even mentions the physical part of yoga, it is meant just to relax and focus you for the 'real' meditation. But as I showed above, the ENTIRE class is really a form of meditation. Having the still after the moving meditation theoretically supercharges the still meditation by allowing you to pay more attention with less distracting thoughts.

A good metaphor of the mind and yoga's effect on it comes from the same book. Imagine the mind is a lake. At the bottom of the lake is a treasure, the real YOU. But you can't see it because of the waves and debris on the lake's surface, like those thoughts about your taxes. Yoga and (aren't they the same thing?) meditation still the surface of the lake/mind so you can see the real you.

A physiologic explanation for this exists as well. Basic neurophysiology says that the brain is changeable. The more you do something, the more neurons are used for it and the firmer and more extensive the connections get that allow you to do it. The reverse is true. Use it or lose it. The same thing applies to learning languages & for the same reason. At its base, meditation of any kind is practicing paying attention to what is happening NOW, not tomorrow when you have a bad meeting with the boss, not when you were a kid and mommy didn't buy you a Betsy Wets Herself doll (really did exist- look it up). This means the nerve tracts for attention get stronger the more you meditate. This has been proven with PET scans, etc. In novice meditators meditating 3x/week for only 8 weeks you can see changes in brain function. Imagine how it is for someone like the Dalai Lama. The lizard brain and the base of the human brain look more or less like your thumb. It deals with purely instinctual reactions like the 4 Fs: Feeding, Fighting, Fleeing & Fornicating. The top of the human brain looks kinda like a walnut. And just like a walnut, it is wrinkled on the outside to pack as much surface area as possible into a finite amount of real estate. The top of the brain is what allows us to be human and do all the non-lizardie things we do. Including selfless behavior, restraint and willingly suffering (school, taxes, compromise, etc.) for a long-term goal. Despite all this we still engage in way too much F-ing (of all the big 4) for our own good. The foundation of the brain is still the lizard brain after all. But as I said before meditation (which can come in many forms, even running your rosary, repeating the 99 names of god, etc.) strengthens the top of the brain tracts used in paying attention to the NOW. This means you are less likely to have a snap lizard brain reaction to whatever comes your way. And more likely to notice when you do. Not a bad thing.

Meditation is also proven to be about as effective as psychotherapy and antidepressants for anxiety and depression. Somewhat similar brain scan changes can be seen after all three. It makes sense too, if you spend hours focusing on what you are feeling now and attempting to be accepting and non-judgmental about whatever comes up, you get better at it. It is the opposite of repeatedly circling back to the Betsy Wets Herself incident that scarred you for life or worrying about how your boss might fire you tomorrow. And the more you do anything the better you get at it. Arnold Schwarzenegger didn't get like he looked in his prime watching reruns on TV. It took hours of weightlifting and tons of 'roids. You can Pump Up the healthier parts of your brain. If you do the work.

Another brain hack from yoga involves something called the homunculus. Homunculus literally means 'little man' in Latin. Besides trying to turn lead into gold and live forever, the medieval alchemists were trying to create little Mini Me-like creatures called homunculi using black magic. There is a part of the brain called the homunculus as well. About midway on each side of the brain there are 2 areas facing each other that control motion and sensation for the corresponding half of the body. If you count the number of neurons in each, there are more neurons for motion and feeling in places that do more of it and less in places that do less for obvious reasons. If you were to use these numbers to make a little man, he would look pretty funky. Big lips, tongue, face, hands and genitals. Small everything else. Take a look on Google images under homunculus & get back to me. And since very few people are truly ambidextrous, not to mention any physical injuries or limitations, the right and left sides of the freaky little guy would be a little unequal. But since yoga is about paying attention to the sensations in your body at a fine level of detail and getting better at moving and holding your body down to a very precise level of detail, yoga could likely even up the 2 sides of the homunculus. And make the parts most people don't have much control over or sensation in, like the low back, better represented in the little guy as you get better at feeling and controlling them. Never mind the strengthening, flexibility, balance etc. you get from yoga, that's pretty cool and interesting. Who knows what that would do for you, but it can't be bad?

And that's just a few of the provable benefits you can see from meditation and (?) yoga. It can get easy pretty fast to venture into all kinds of mystical benefits, but then you would need to believe in a soul …

I don't need to believe in a soul, I believe in yoga.

IT'S A WONDER DRUG!

digitalize: Verb. To administer digitalis or digoxin to (a patient with a heart complaint).

-Dictionary definition

Digitalis is a very old drug. It is originally from the foxglove plant. Van Gogh has a famous painting of his doctor holding a foxglove flower. He was getting it for his bipolar (?) disorder. Doesn't work for that unfortunately. But it might have influenced some of his paintings. It *can* turn your vision yellow or make you see halos around lights. Take a look on Google under VG *Sunflowers* or *Starry Night* and get back to me. It can slow the heart rate down if it is too fast and make it pump a little stronger. It is still used to this day.

My first rotation in medical school after the classroom years was in surgery. You get put in one of the teams of surgeons and follow them around the hospital during their daily rounds for a month. This involves a lot of walking from room to room seeing patients then talking about their case/plans, etc. after reviewing their latest labs & X-Rays. Surgery (especially on your belly) and the immobility and (constipating) narcotics that go with it tend to block your bowels for a few days afterward. Normally the surgeons are very interested in whether you have had a poop or even gas since the surgery. It is one of the things that determine when you can go home. Normally you can't go home until you've pooped.

One particular patient was a monolingual Korean speaker. He had just had surgery for stomach cancer. Something Koreans are especially prone to due to a diet high in salted fish. And probably a diet high in Marlboro too. Smoking is SUPER common in Korean men. At that point I knew how to say 3 things in Korean: hi, fart & thanks. Every day when we went in to see him, I trotted out my 3 words.

We were all standing around the X-Ray box one day looking at a different patient's belly X-Ray. He was full of shit. Literally. The various residents were talking about him & one said: 'If he doesn't shit soon, we're going to have to digitalize him. My first thought and (unfortunately) the first words out of my mouth were: 'Digitalis?!? I knew the heart stuff, but it helps you poop too?!?'

Needless to say, I was wrong. The guy lifted his hand and used one finger (digit) to show what someone (probably me as I was the low man on the totem pole & as they say: Shit flows downhill) would be doing with said digit to pull the poop out of his rectum if needed. I like to picture & hear the 'shark music' from the movie *Jaws* with an outstretched index finger swimming along to the beat like the shark's dorsal fin. Duh-Dum Dah Dum … This is called **Digital Disimpaction.** You put on some gloves, grab some K-Y and use your finger to hook out one piece at a time. Usually smells really nice too. Everyone had a good laugh & fortunately, I never had to touch his rectum.

I still have to do it on someone every once it in a while.

You think you got a shitty job?

Or your boss always gives you the shittiest assignments?

Or those rich doctors get shitloads of money for talking & writing stuff?

Let's see how you feel about that after you've walked a mile in my gloves up various assholes …

JUST NOT HERE

About 40% of all ER patients do not truly qualify as 'emergencies'.

-medical statistic

The above statistic is just one of the frustrating things about working in the ER. But it is pretty big. There is an epidemic of 'burnout' in doctors and ER docs consistently are some of the worst. People get depressed, bitter, cynical, compassion fatigue and feel their work is useless.

Think about it. Pretty close to half of the people you see in any given shift should not be in an EMERGENCY room of all places. Tons of incurable colds, often the entire family. Tons of 2 mile per hour car accidents trying to build a case for Jacoby & Meyers or some other ambulance chasing (the origin of that term btw) scumbag attorney to make his percentage. I had one mom & infant come to the ER about **3 AM** dressed like she was going to sell herself for $ (and in a way she was) with her mans &/or attorney to both be seen after a minor car accident with no complaints that happened at **5PM**. Not a scratch on either of them & the kid was in a car seat during the accident. Her attorney told her to go to the ER. Of course, I'm pretty sure he didn't tell her to wait until 3 AM. Or to dress like a whore when she did. Nice. Tons of people who forgot how to count &/or use a telephone to call their doctor a week or 2 before their regular prescription ran out. Or the guy who came in because his friend was there for something more legitimate and decided to relieve his boredom by checking in as a patient because his ears were always a little itchy. He hadn't even tried lotion yet. I told him to do so and let him know that his bosses in the Army might be unhappy at him for using government $ on something like this instead of waiting for the base clinic in the am. Some people even call 911 to get an ambulance ride for ridiculous things like a cold. One mom was actually upset when I asked her why she called 911 for the kid's cold at 4 AM. Her answer was of course: 'I didn't have a ride'. Or the person with whatever for 3 months to 15 years. I have said 'The sign out front doesn't say: 6-Month-Old Problem Room.' more times than I can count. Or the homeless who tend to show up with obviously bogus complaints whenever there is a cold snap or heavy rain. In ER lingo their real chief complaint is TCO. Too Cold Outside. Not to mention that a lot of this care (including those $1250-2500 ambulance rides instead of a friend, taxi or Uber), usually comes out of my taxes as a high percentage of these visits are by the publicly insured.

I keep trying to remind myself that a lot of these people are too limited & common sense is too uncommon to prevent them from coming in. And of course, our social safety net is pretty tattered. And people's regular doctors, if they have them, are often booked weeks in advance.

But that is just the tip of the iceberg that gets shoved up my rectum on a regular basis. There are always lots of people who come in just to get high &/or (ideally &) a nice narcotic Rx to take at home or sell. They think they are so clever about it. But they all say the same things. Hospitals are required to rate a patient's pain level & give medicine for their pain. Most of the time the nurses ask them to rate their pain as 1-10 on a 10-point scale. It has been proven that people who are drug- seeking consistently call their pain 10/10 or even 11/10. This and the overall drama factor with a general tendency to overrate pain for faster attention are why most doctors don't ask for X/10 but say 'mild, moderate or severe?' They usually are 'allergic' to all but the most mental high inducing pain meds. Their doctor is often 'outta town'. They 'lost or got robbed of their pills'. They of course are special and 'need' only the narcotics that give you the best high at twice the normal maximum dose. Sometimes they will bring in 5 or 10-year-old X-rays to show you how bad their back is. One of the latest drug crazes is cough syrup, popularized in multiple rap songs. I have been told the street value of a bottle of certain prescription cough syrups is up to $300. One of my colleagues is such a light touch that all the professional drug addicts show up on his regular days on. There was even a fight in the ER between two groups of kids looking for cough sizzurp (one of the street names for cough syrup) with over a dozen people total involved. It is so common that there are multiple animated videos with titles similar to 'drug seeking patient in ER' on YouTube. Look it up now on your phone, etc. & get back to me ...

Wasn't that fun? Imagine seeing that person (or his/her many clones) up to 8 times in a 12-hour shift.

Then there are the alcoholics who come in up to several times a day because they passed out on the sidewalk and some innocent bystander called 911. Once they get to the ER, they have to stay sometimes over 12 hours until they are sober enough to leave. Some will come in because they are drunk and want to get sober. Unfortunately, there is nothing most ERs without a rehab section of the hospital can do about besides tell them to go to AA. Of course, drunk people do things like get naked, scream, ask the same? 50 times, pee on the floor, vomit or poop on themselves. Nice. Similarly, people freaking out on drugs will often come in, usually with the police who want to get rid of them ASAP. This is why I have a heavy hand on sedating them early to let them sleep it off without incident.

Or people on psychiatric holds, who can sometimes stay in the ER for up to a week waiting for a psychiatric hospital to have a bed for them. Again, not the most pleasant people as a general rule. And when you ask them, often they aren't taking their psych meds, are talking drugs and alcohol and not going to AA. And some of them get admitted to a psych hospital for feeling 'suicidal' 3 times a week. I understand free food, clothing and shelter are kinda nice. And conveniently enough, it has been shown that back when they used to release disability checks the first of the month, there were drastically more psychiatric hospitalizations at the end of the month. That is why they stagger the checks now.

And again, alcoholics, drug addicts and the mentally ill aren't likely to have insurance paid for at any expense but yours. Of course, all the above are not entirely in control of their actions. But if you don't even try to go to AA or take your psych meds, it makes it a lot harder to care about you.

And of course, a vast number of patients are there because of their own actions. You get drunk, fall down, go boom, get cut or broke and then act like a nasty loudmouthed drunk when you get in the ER. You smoke for 50 years when the government has spent billions and everyone around you has been telling you not to and end up with cancer, emphysema, a heart attack or a stroke. You eat McDonalds every day while never exercising and end up with diabetes, high blood pressure, high cholesterol, heart attacks, strokes or kidney failure. Again, my taxes pay for a lot of your shenanigans. Dialysis for kidney failure costs $6000 per month for the rest of your, from that point on, short life.

Lastly, due to all the factors I mentioned above as well as just plain bad parenting, people tend to be at their worst in the ER. Especially at night. I have been screamed at, insulted or even physically threatened more times than I can count. I have seen more 'adult men' drag their mommies in with them or make them pick them up at 3 in the morning because they got drunk or high than I could even try to estimate. I have had people who complain to administration because they weren't seen fast enough. Who cares if 3 people were literally dying and they were in the ER for chapped lips?

Buddhism teaches that very few people are actually intentionally 'evil.' They are trying to do what they think is right but can't because their mom was a rabid wolf who put out cigarettes on their butt or whatever the specifics may be. But try to get there when a drunk is screaming at you.

This is perfectly illustrated by the case of a friend of mine from a hospital I used to work at. He took a job as a registration/admitting clerk at the ER of a hospital in a largely Chinese area of LA right after getting his bachelor's degree. He is Chinese American himself and figured it would be an easy job where he could help his people while getting ready for grad school. Very nice, smart kid who had more school and was smarter by far than his co-workers or boss. But a little naïve and didn't know what he was getting into.

After he had been there 6 months or so, another friend asked him: 'So are you still optimistic about humanity?'

His answer sums up this entire story: **'I'm still optimistic about humanity, just not here.'**

I keep trying to remind myself that most all these people are doing the best the can, just that their best isn't very good. But ... This is why I now work full time as a hospitalist at a local cancer (only) hospital with ER only a few nights a month to keep my certification up.

JUST SAY NO TO METH

Getting involved in the world of meth, I've got a chance to meet some very, ahem, *interesting* people. Most of whom, if you saw them on fire on the other side of the street, you wouldn't cross the street to piss on them to put the fire out.

-part of the opening monologue to the movie *The Salton Sea*

All the hard drugs are bad. Heroin and opiates have terrible withdrawals and are easy to accidentally OD with, not to mention all the issues if you shoot up. Coke is very addictive and can kill you and wears off fast so you always need MORE. Valium etc. can also kill you and withdrawal can last up to a year.

Meth is an entirely different animal. It is relatively cheap and the high can last up to 3 days. Imagine that. Most people get a little off after one night without sleep. And since meth is a stimulant, you aren't sleeping for days. And that assumes you do it once and then take a break. It's not very hard to stay awake for a week or two on meth. People are rumored to have been awake for a year or more with meth. You get hyper alert and have all this energy to burn. People have been known to spend 3 hours readjusting their sock drawer to get it just right. Imagine what you can do to your face if you start picking a zit. That is why using meth is called tweaking and meth heads are also called tweakers. Go to Faces of Meth on Google and get back to me. Pretty, no? I like to talk about Marlboro years and people's faces. Kinda like dog years. Dogs supposedly age 7 times as fast as we do; so, a 1 one-year old dog is equivalent to a 7-year-old person and so on. Meth years are drastically worse than Marlboro years. And most meth heads do both. If you're gonna do something as dumb as meth, do you really think that cigarette pack warning is gonna faze you?

But it doesn't stop there, meth gives you a huge sustained bump in dopamine. This is also raised in schizophrenics. Both can cause you to get paranoid and see or hear things. It can be impossible to tell a meth head from a schizophrenic without getting the real story or a drug test. Hitler was a meth head. His doctors were giving the 'glorious' fuhrer shots of the newly discovered wonder drug amphetamine to give him extra energy for his 'important' work.

One thing, in particular, is infamous among meth heads. The technical term is formication. M not N there. It refers to the poison in an ant sting, formic acid, related to formaldehyde as in the morgue. More commonly it is known as coke bugs or **meth bugs**. Coke & meth can both cause it, but since meth lasts so much longer, it is more common with meth. You get the feeling there are bugs under your skin and sometimes even see them. Sounds like a good reason to do meth, no? Obviously pretty distressing & probably accounts for a lot of the skin picking meth heads do. There is now a Dr. Google diagnosis called Morgellon's disease. It does not exist. There are no bugs in North America that do anything even remotely close to that. The medical diagnosis is called delusional parasitosis. Every medical society says this is purely a psychiatric phenomenon caused by drugs or mental illness. Try explaining that to a meth head. Impossible.

And then the teeth. Super Pretty. Some combination of dry mouth from the meth (like when you get scared by a lion jumping in front of you but lasting up to 3 days or more), teeth grinding from being so amped, sugary drinks to fight the dry mouth & just plain sucking toxic chemicals past your teeth does bad things to them teeth. Most meth heads end up toothless before long. One woman (definitely not a *lady*) I saw came in because her teeth hurt. When I looked in there, every single tooth had the enamel peeling off like wallpaper that got wet then dried on the front & back side of the tooth. No solution to that as far as I can tell besides pull them all out.

One case report tells of a guy who ended up in the ER wacked out of his head. He got admitted and eventually came around. Then they found him on the floor wacked again. And he got better and then was found wacked in the stairwell. At this point they figured out he had a bottle of liquid meth and a pack of tampons. He would soak the tampon in the meth & shove it up his ass. The next time he came around he eloped from the hospital. Probably dead by now, I'm sure.

In my psych rotation in internship, we had one patient who seemed like a classic schizophrenic. The 'Church' of Scientology was harassing him to join because his wife and whole family had already joined up. Plausible so far. I made the mistake of filling out a survey of theirs once and get mail from them for over 5 years after, despite never replying or giving them a forwarding address. Then his story started to go off the rails. They had a listening device in his ear & sometimes used it to tell him things. He was picked up by the police because he held up a guy at Dennys, who was in on the plot of course, with a comb in his pocket to look like a gun. He was only trying to get him to tell the truth about the Scientology plot. But he's OK; he just wants us to give him a paper saying the Scientology guys are harassing him. He's got a wife, a house, he has his own business. Then we found out the truth. **No one** is into Scientology. He went off the deep end on meth, lost his business and wife and the family is afraid of him.

Another guy kept coming to the ER because of the rats. He had a rat phobia. And a serious meth habit. And kept hallucinating that the rats were in his stomach trying to eat their way out. That's why his stomach kept hurting … Even after several ER visits for the belly and tons of tests, he could not get it out of his head that it was the rats. I gave him a little antipsychotic med and told him he needed to get into AA or else.

A young once pretty girl kept coming in because of the spiders. She was a meth head and heroin addict who smoked. Once you add up all those frequent flier miles on her face, you can imagine how fast & how ugly things got. Not too long ago she had even lost an eye. Every time I saw her, I told her: 'No, it's not spiders in your hair; it's the meth like I've told you at least a half dozen times already.' Some of my more clueless colleagues kept giving her meds for lice, etc. Last time I saw her she had upgraded from spiders to rats chasing her. As always, she got a little anticrazy meds and left still trying to convince me it was rats not meth.

LET'S GET IT ON!

I've been really tryin', baby
Tryin' to hold back this feeling for so long
And if you feel like I feel, baby
Then, c'mon, oh, c'mon
Let's get it on
Ah, baby, let's get it on
Let's love, baby
Let's get it on

-from *Let's Get It On* by Marvin Gaye

The ER is supposed to be for emergencies only. Not primary care. An ER doctor is not anybody's Primary Care Doctor. But things don't always work out that way. For whatever reason, some people keep coming so often that you get to know them in some ways more than some of your own family members. There are dozens of people who as soon as I see them or the name, I can tell you the highlights of their medical issues and personalities. This is rarely a good thing. Either they are alcoholics or drug addicts or just so sick that they have to come back all the time. Sometimes though, regular nice people who are doing all the right things end up being frequent fliers because of holes in the social safety net or long waits to get into their PMD.

One of these ladies I'll call Amanda. She was in her late 20s & a single mom with a few kids. Always nice and never abused to system coming to the ER for true BS, at least not more than taking her kids to the ER for the common cold. I ended up seeing her and her kids so often we would joke about how I was their PMD. She was such a sweet lady with well-behaved kids that it was always a pleasure to have her as a patient.

One of the first times I saw her she must have had a urine infection because I had to examine her belly. Right at the level of her pelvis she had a tattoo saying: 'LET'S GET IT ON!' Might explain her having those kids. I didn't ever bring it up with her because I didn't want to embarrass her, but every time I saw her, I had a little mental smile thinking about her naughty little secret.

Last time I saw her & had to do an exam, the tattoo was faded and halfway to being burned off.

For the best. How would she have explained **that** to the kids once they got old enough to read …?

MASTER OF NONE

Jack of all trades, master of none. <u>Figure of Speech.</u> used in reference to a person who has dabbled in many skills, rather than gaining expertise by focusing on one.

-Wikipedia definition

The above saying is often applied to ER doctors since they 'have no specialty'. This despite the fact that an ER residency takes at least 3 years and Emergency Medicine has been an official specialty for over 40 years. One of the questions I hear all the time after telling someone that I am an ER doctor is '& what's your specialty?' There is some validity to this of course. Most medical specialties are offshoots of Internal Medicine or Surgery. Stuff like Psychiatry or Radiology are obviously things on their own. Emergency Medicine means you have to know enough of all the specialties to take care of anyone who walks or is carried in the door. But I'm not going to do any real surgery, although I can do more minor surgical procedures than anybody but a surgeon. I'm not going to do an angiogram and put in a stent if you have a heart attack, but I can do most any other cardiac stuff. I am trained to deliver babies if I have too, but I'd rather leave that to an OB (and his or her malpractice insurance) if at all possible. And I can put a dislocated shoulder back in place pretty damn good but I'm not gonna put pins or rods in a badly broken bone. I am very good at intubating you if you can't breathe, but I'm not gonna sit at your bedside giving anesthesia during a surgery. I can sew pretty well, but still call in a plastic surgeon for a complicated cut on the face, especially on a young lady.

There are things that essentially no other specialty does besides ER. Disaster medicine and Emergency Medical Services are usually run by ER docs. Toxicology is also something which we are the only ones who really get training in. And Wilderness Medicine with all the various bites and exposures are something we do that most docs don't.

There are things we don't do also that almost every other doctor does do. Like hiring, firing, owning and paying for an office, fighting with insurance companies and paying for our own malpractice insurance. And almost every doctor out there does the same thing every day. Get up at 5 to be at the hospital to see your patients who are already there. Go to the office and see patients all day there or do surgery. Go back to the hospital to see what happened to your people from the morning and anyone you sent in during the day. Go home and potentially answer pages all nite from the local ER or about your admitted patients. On Saturday they may even be open for a half day at the office. Regardless, they are still going to the hospital Saturday and Sunday if they have anyone admitted. This can be made easier if you give away some or all of your call &/or hospital duties to a partner or outside group, but then you are giving away $.

I learned early on that ER was for me. I am a little restless and don't like to sit still without doing something. My dad calls me 'Nervous' as a nickname. Fortunately, I love to read, so sitting still is rarely a problem unless I forget to bring a book. My college had a class for pre-meds where we got to spend a semester observing doctors in the hospital and doing minor things like taking BPs. Later we got a letter and of course experience in health care to help in applying to med school.

The first semester everyone 'had' to be in the ER. Fast paced, always something new coming in the door, endless variety, all kinds of procedures going on. What's not to love? I vividly remember doing CPR the first time ever on this guy with a blue face who was essentially dead already. And a guy who had practically cut his thumb off, it was only attached by a thin strip of skin. The doc on duty cut the skin, threw the thumb in a bucket and closed the skin over the stub. I spent the rest of the procedure watching the thumb sitting there in the bucket looking lonely. When a patient had to go to the OR, I followed them up and was mesmerized looking at the intestines moving slowly like giant worms. And in between patients the docs could read, eat and talk. Cool.

The second semester was open to several different specialties and we got to pick in order determined by a lottery. I never win stuff like that, but this time I did. Since everyone wanted to see OB and the whole 'miracle of life' thing, I picked that. Big mistake, at least for me. Unless you consider learning that I did NOT want to do OB a good thing. That part was definitely true.

In the first month I saw several deliveries. But they always ended the same way. Ugh, Ugh, scream, Ugh push, baby comes out or they go to get a C-section. Either way, they often got an epidural for pain. A needle is inserted near the spine & anesthesia is put in. It seemed like every one of the 5 or so I saw was done by the same anesthesiologist. He was 'old.' Which probably means about my age or even as ancient as 60ish. Either way, he had been doing this for a good 20 or 30 years. Thousands of epidurals. And every time he gave the same speech, word for word. 'I'm going to put a needle in the small of your back, and then put in some medicine, you may feel ...' Uncountable times. Word for Word. If that was me, I would have put a gun to my head within a few years. No wonder anesthesiologists have some of the highest rates of drug abuse among doctors. As they say 'hours of boredom & minutes of terror.' I dropped the class after the first month. **Boooring ...**

One of my professors was a foregut surgeon. This meant he did surgery from the throat to a little past the stomach. I at first thought he was a genius because he would assign all the students in his group a few articles on heartburn surgery. He even knew the page numbers in the journal. Later I realized he had been doing this parlor trick for years. And it's easy to remember the articles pertinent to your specialty when there are 8 of them (not true of course, but you get the point).

His favorite saying, tellingly, was: 'There are no boring jobs, just boring people.' I beg to differ. In fact, I could say that someone who could be happy doing the same 10 or so operations for 30 or 40 years sounds pretty boring in my book. Not that I don't want those people around, they have their place. Of course, you could counter that I am just shallow and can't appreciate the infinite shades of subtle variations that exist between each case with any given operation and can't appreciate the way I get incrementally better each time, blah, blah, blah ...

Are you still talking?

I stopped paying attention years ago.

MEN CAN BE BITCHES TOO

Yo, how did he go out?
He went out like a bitch!
So ladies
We ain't just talkin' bout you
Cause some of you n****s
Is bitches too!

Partial lyrics from *bitches 2* by Ice-T

I have seen 'Rosa Maria' dozens of times. She has chronic back pain, which is very real and caused by multiple bad discs, etc. She is also at least a former meth addict, still smokes and last time I looked her up in the state of California's prescribed drug (narcotic) history website had received at least 1500-2000 pills of various narcotics in the last calendar year. Unlike many of my colleagues, as can be seen by the sheer number of pills she gets prescribed, I never give her anything more than 2 pills of vicodin & a non-narcotic pain shot. I never give her a Rx as she has way too many pills already & tell her to go to or call her MD in the AM for more if she needs them. She is always there with her husband, who also smokes but as far as I can tell, doesn't so any drugs. She has had a hard life and has several gang tattoos. She has told me in the past how she beat her stepdad up when he was treating her bad. She has been to jail for various things a few times.

Because I always treat her with respect but have firm boundaries with her, she likes me. I am on a first name basis with her and her husband. I have talked her through issues they have had together often caused by her acting out. She got sentenced to domestic violence classes for hitting him once. And I tell her that she needed to get into AA to work through all the bad stuff in her past to make sure she didn't relapse and to help her keep an even keel with her husband, etc. And it might even help her with the chronic pain. As far as I can tell she never tried that hard to go there. I have always told her she needs to stop hanging out with the Marlboro Man because that makes her back, ulcer and emphysema worse. Once when she actually had for a while (before falling off the wagon into an ashtray), I told her that her hair smelled terrific, like in the old commercials, when I bumped into her in the cafeteria. She made it a point to introduce me to her friends there. Of course, I also tease the husband about stopping hanging out with Paul Mall (yes, I know how it is supposed to be spelled). Whenever she comes in, she is always happy to see me, as is her hubby. We spend a little time catching up. I even went to birthday alarm once when she was in on her birthday & showed her an e-card for her big day.

Another drug seeking patient was coming in regularly for a while. He wasn't even necessarily looking to get high, but wanted attention or just a bed for the night or if he hit the jackpot, to get admitted. He has chronic shoulder pain and never needed anything besides a onetime dose of some non-narcotic pain meds (at your tax $s expense, of course). Regardless, he would refuse to leave and was a real jackass every time. His ER visits usually led to him being kicked out by security or even having the police called if he truly refused to leave after getting what he needed but not what he wanted. In the words of the great British philosopher Keith Richards: 'you don't always get what you want, but sometimes, if you try real hard, you get what you need'. As the first person giving him the bad news that he had to get out, he often got confrontational and tried to intimidate me. I don't intimidate easy. And I know that manipulative people can sense fear and will use that to their advantage. There are classes which ER and psych medical staff are forced to take about how to deal with physically assaultive patients. The biggest thing they teach you is to keep your distance and try to anticipate what they might do next.

Anytime I have heard about a fellow staff member being assaulted by a patient, it is always the person who comes off as weakest or meekest or most trusting out of the crew on at that particular time. This is not an accident. Since I didn't back down, his volume went up and once he even got out of bed and tried to really puff himself up (not very effective when I have a good 6" in height on him). On that occasion he told me 'You want to see what I'm made of?' I restrained myself from replying that I already knew and detailing some of what I knew. He never gave up and eventually I would tell him he WAS leaving whether he wanted to or not and walk out on him mid-tantrum. Then it became the nurses' job, then security, then more often than not the PD.

The first time I saw him he had signed out Against Medical Advice from County Hospital where he was admitted for his chronic shoulder pain because they weren't taking care of him in the manner to which he wanted to be accustomed. At least that's his story. Maybe he did actually talk some chump into admitting him when he didn't need it. There's a sucker born every minute. And a coward. My predecessor signed him out to me after some pain meds and an un-needed X-ray because she knew she didn't have it in her to get him to leave and that I did. I left him fuming and turned his discharge over to the RN, then security then ...

Right about then Rosa was checking in. Since she knows every local ER better than she does her own house, she let herself in and went to the bathroom which is right next to his bed. She couldn't help but to overhear his rant about this Dr. Wade being such an asshole, etc. She diverted to his bed and told him to shut up, that Dr. Wade is cool. His rant then went her direction. He started speaking in tongues and shaking his cane at her. She flipped the switch and went off on him. She shook her cane at him and gave him the Don't Fuck With Me look. He sat down & shut up. She then told him; 'Say you're my bitch!'. He promptly complied. When the police got there, they took him away and I made sure they knew he was guilty of assault for threatening some 'poor lady' patient with his cane. Sometimes the world just plain works out the way it should.

I didn't hear about the 'say you're my bitch!' part for weeks after it happened but it is the icing on the cake ...

In the words of some goofball country 'music' singer: 'I've got friends in low places'.

MILITARY INTELLIGENCE

Oxymoron: Noun. A combination of <u>contradictory</u> or incongruous words (such as *cruel kindness*).

-Webster's dictionary definition

Since I ended up going to a school AKA University of Spoiled Children for medical school, I had to find a way to get it paid for since I am far from a spoiled children and at the time it cost $25K per year *just* for tuition. Not to mention books, equipment and fees. Nor food, clothing and shelter. A friend of mine was in the Air Force before school and suggested I try that. They have a program where they pay for school, etc. and give you enough to live on during school. In return you spend a month a year with them. The summer after the first year of school you do your basic training. Since you are a college graduate, you are already an officer you don't get screamed at by the drill instructors and have maids to clean your dorm room. Later you do a few of your hospital rotations at AF hospitals. After school you owe them 4 years as a doctor. The recruiter I talked to told me: 'We want our doctors to be happy so we try to do whatever we can as far as getting them assignments they like, etc.' and showed me brochures with bases in the Greek islands and Italy. And the Air Force is the least military of the services and by definition is not on the front lines in a war.

Sounds like a deal, no? But I didn't realize what I learned later again & again. Recruiters LIE!

The first warning signs came at boot camp. Yes, we did get treated better than the enlisted or the Officer Training Corps guys. We shared the same cafeteria with the OTC chumps. They had to walk like robots in line to get lunch. If they did one single thing wrong, it was worse than the Soup Nazi from *Seinfeld*: 'No Soup (or anything) For You!' Speaking of walking, I could barely do it. I had just gotten out of a cast for a broken leg with no weight bearing for 3 ½ months less than a month before. And my dumbass orthopedist never sent me to physical therapy. I am still trying to get my right side to be as flexible etc. over 25 years later, the last 11 of which I have been doing yoga regularly. This was a big problem as marching and running are a big part of boot camp. I came with a doctor's note and wasn't malingering at all, but still was a marked man from the start. The Japanese have a saying: 'The nail which sticks up will be pounded down.' The same applies to the military. Then I have a tendency to not want to do stupid shit that makes no sense to me. And asking stupid questions like: 'Why?' or 'What's the point of marching?' Patriarchal systems where orders are given and not expected to be questioned don't like that.

These took a turn for the Orwellian in the last week. We had a class called: 'Psychological Motivation of Troops.' The instructor told us how there are 2 curves they apply to new people: 1 of how much pressure you put on them and another of their responsibility (in doing what YOU want) level. When they start out you put a lot of pressure on them, as they get more trustworthy you start taking it away. It is similar to the way they train an elephant. When it is a baby, you put a heavy chain on it. By the time it grows up, you only need a thin string. It is also known as **brainwashing**. I think I was one of the only ones there who realized the full implications of this. First, they had been doing this to US. Second, they now thought that they had turned us into such mindless drones that we could be taught to do it to other people. At the end of boot camp my instructor told me: 'You really need to decide if you want to stay in the AF.' Since I was still in need of tuition and figured it couldn't be too bad once I got out of residency & was working for the Air Farce as an ER doc somewhere, I decided to stay in. Stupid me.

Near the end of medical school, I applied for a civilian residency (rather than one with the AF which adds extra time onto your sentence and means that many more years wearing polyester and saluting) and was only given 1 year for internship. Halfway through internship I took a physical and applied to finish my residency at the place I was already at. They said no, I 'got' to be a general practitioner and could apply for where I wanted to go. General practitioners are something that died somewhere about the late 50s in the civilian world. Even to do something relatively easy like Family Medicine you need to complete a 3-year residency. Medicine is much more complicated than it used to be and a basic internship is not enough for any but a few exceptional individuals with limited practices to do safely or well anymore. And I was an ER intern anyway, so even less prepared to handle being in an office seeing family practice patients. But the Air Farce doesn't know anything besides planes. A pilot is a pilot, right? But they wouldn't let someone with a basic pilot certification fly a multimillion $ jet fighter without lots of extra training. But then people are cheaper and more expendable than planes. And military patients can't sue for malpractice. And as they are fond of saying: 'We defend the constitution, we don't have to follow it.' My year was THE last year in which they had doctors with nothing but an internship as general practitioners. They finally got smarter, but too late to save me from 2 years, 7 months, 11 days & 11 ½ hours in Hell.

Needless to say I was pissed. ER residencies are pretty competitive, if they didn't let me finish, odds were high I would never be able to get back into ER. It got even better when some incompetent boob lost my physical exam, so I had to reapply for locations after everyone else after redoing the physical. I got onto the request list late & ended up getting one of the 2 worst locations in the entire US, Del Rio TX. A small town in the middle of nowhere on the border. I hate heat, Texas and small towns. The place with the most alcohol related incidents in the Air Farce. Hell on Earth.

I wrote my congressman & tried everything I could to get out. I even told them I was gay. My dad talked to a military attorney who said that if I didn't take that back & they investigated; I could go to Leavenworth Federal Prison. Fortunately, they didn't do anything once I recanted. I got there late the nite before I was supposed to show up. I didn't have time or care for that matter to iron my uniform before reporting for duty so showed up wrinkled. And got my first counseling. At first I tried to comply at least until I reapplied in the fall to go back to residency & was told no f**kin' way.

Then I went all out. I was intentionally sloppy with my uniform, which is the way I roll anyway. I don't buy shirts that need ironing. Eventually I was made to have my clothes professionally ironed or get charged with disobeying a direct order which again means Leavenworth. I always let my hair grow at as long as I could until I was told I needed a haircut, despite wanting a very short haircut to go with the punk rock crowd I hung with. I ended up getting more write-ups than I can count. My file of them was about as thick as a medium size town's phone book. At one point my boss told me: 'You are not getting out of here before June 26, 2000 unless you go to Leavenworth.' I was fined and had bonuses withheld and was even unable to leave the town for 6 months.

One of my favorites was for improper use of the in-house email system. One of the other docs was unhappy with the place too, but on a much lower level than me. She sent out a minor gripe about the place. I agreed and she asked what I would do to fix it. I replied with a version of something a friend said about my previous hospital to all the docs and nurses on the system (including my boss a nurse & Lieutenant Colonel): 'Burn the place to the ground. Bulldoze the rubble. Salt the earth so that nothing can ever grow there again. Brand anyone over the rank of Technical Sergeant or Major with the Mark of Cian (typo for CAIn) on the forehead so they can be recognized wherever they go for the rest of their lives.' She loved it. My boss not so much. When I got called into his office and asked for an explanation, I apologized for the typo.

The Air Farce tends to be hypocritical when it suits them. They talk about how drunk driving and smoking is bad but let you buy them at subsidized low prices on base. Similarly, they take a hard line on asthma as a disqualifying condition. Flying in small unpressurized planes and not being able to breathe, makes sense. But if you are already in when you get officially diagnosed, especially if you owe them time like I did, they will just say you can't be stationed overseas. I have had bad allergies my whole life. In med school asthma got added to the mix but it was never officially diagnosed until the Air Farce. Another legit medical issue that was inconvenient for the Air Farce. Easy solution, you stay in.

The Air Farce likes to have you sign papers saying you know not to do stupid shit so if you do, they got you where they want you. And in peacetime even big people like the base commander for a pilot training base don't have much useful to do. Our guy was Colonel Winterburger, but he was such a tool that everyone on base called him Weenieburger. And he was a micromanaging pinhead.

They make a big deal about 'the 100 days of summer' because that is when they get the most DUIs. The Weenie went around the whole base having people sign a set of papers saying 'I know drunk driving bad, calling people bad names bad …' He came to the clinic lobby as I was coming out front to get my next patient. He asked me 'Captain (because that is SOOO much more of an important difficult title to get than Doctor, ya know) Wade have you signed these yet?' I took the clipboard and saw what it was. I asked him in front of a lobby full of patients and staff 'So basically I can't drink & drive or call anyone bad names?' He cheerfully replied 'And no sexual harassment.' This was my cue to say while looking disappointed and raising my voice: 'No sexual harassment?!? No sexual harassment?!? What am I going to do with the afternoon now?!? I already made plans!?!' Then I signed it without reading anything, tossed it on the counter and walked back to my office. My proudest moment in the Air Farce. I heard about that for months.

I saw one of the base attorneys as a patient once. And they only had prosecutors on base. We were too small a base to have attorneys to defend us. She told me how they were all amused in her office at my creativity.

The final straw came from the magic of the internet. There used to be a satirical page that purported to be Jesus homepage & blog before such a word existed. 'Hi my name is Jesus, I am the savior of a major World religion, in my free time I like to drink wine with my friends, go out boating and hang out with prostitutes …' It had a place where you could email Jesus. So I did. In the satirical, blasphemous manner of the site. Title: 'About last nite' Body: 'You were the best f**k I ever had!' Pretty sure you can figure out what the asterisks are for. I thought it was pretty funny. Never found out what Jesus thought about it though because the base NetNanny program stopped it and sent it to my boss.

When my trial type thing came around, it started to look like they might not kick me out because I hadn't gotten into much trouble since then. I asked my attorney for a recess so I could tell him to do whatever it took to get me out under any terms. He said not to worry & showed me the latest Air Farce legal magazine about how this horrible doctor was making the entire division of the Air Farce look bad & needed to be kicked out before he turned any other apples rotten.

After the whole thing my old boss had gotten into trouble himself and instead of a promotion and a better next spot, he got a congressional investigation for abuse of power started by his former Sergeant/hatchet man and sent to another shithole in the middle of nowhere.

There is a Doctor Seuss story called *Yertle the Turtle*. King Yertle is king of all he can see, which is a pond full of turtles. Oh boy. So, he decides to make all the turtles stand on each other's backs so he can use them for a throne and have so much more to see and therefore be king of. The guy at the bottom of the turtle throne, Mack, gets tired of this fast. He tries to tell king Yertle: 'I've got pains in my back, shoulders and knees. Let me out please!' Yertle is too busy looking at his new kingdom to care. So, Mack shrugs his shoulders and Yertle falls face first into the mud. He can see nothing but mud, so is the King of Mud.

As soon as I escaped, I got my haircut super short to show up on the last day. And sent a copy of *Yertle* to my old boss and his equally nasty successor. I put Sergeant Mack on the return address for his copy. And a nice gift note that said: 'June 26, 2000, my ass! Hope you enjoy middle of nowhere New Mexico! Congressional investigations are a bitch ...'

MY BUDDY PUTIN

Retreat? Is there no gunpowder left in our powder horns?

-from the short story *Taras Bulba* by Nikolai Gogol

I went to Russia twice. The first time was in 2004. The last (for quite a while-more on why later) in 2012. Russia has always fascinated me. Probably from growing up in the cold war. Quite literally we were one mixed message away from starting a 2-sided nuclear war. And as the old saying goes: An eye for an eye blinds the whole world. It would have been the end of the world as we know it. Fortunately Trump and his mouth weren't anywhere near being president then or …

After the fall of the Iron Curtain, things got safer for everyone and more interesting. The LA Times started a series of in-depth articles about Russia and its culture & history which was a good primer. My personal reading plan quickly turned into something of an obsession with the Russian writers. They talk of what to us is quite an exotic, unknown place and culture. And the Russian character tends to go to extremes. As one of the best Russian writers, Dostoevski, said: 'If a Russian were to become a Catholic, he would become the most fanatical Jesuit.' And many of the Russian writers are obsessed with the big themes of life. All this leads to some pretty exciting reading. Much better than much of the staid, stiff upper lip Victorian British and American writing. Those guys bored me so badly that I swore off English & American writers for years in favor of the Russians and French.

And of course, after reading so much about Russia, I was dying to go there and see the place firsthand. I went for a week with my first wife on my first trip. After reading so much about St. Petersburg, I was expecting it to be my favorite city there. It is built on canals like Amsterdam or Venice largely in a French style. To my disappointment, it was too European for me and seemed like a knockoff of Western European architecture. We went to Peter the Great's palace outside the city. While quite pretty and impressive, it seemed too much like the palace of Versailles built by the French kings outside Paris. Even the world-famous Hermitage Museum wasn't that exciting to me. While it has some interesting Western European art stolen from the Nazis at the end of the war after the Nazis stole it from everywhere else and some interesting royal trinkets from the old rulers the czars, it seemed too much like the Louvre to me. While there one of our fellow museum goers fell and hit his head and was bleeding. I introduced myself as a doctor and offered to take a look. I was shocked to be asked for my medical license by the guy. Apparently generations of mistrust of authorities doesn't wear off that fast.

Moscow ended up being my real favorite of the 2 Russian capitals. It seemed more like the real Russia to me. All the onion domed churches, the Kremlin seat of government and Red Square (Actually a mistranslation. It was meant to be called Beautiful Square in Russian but the words for Red and Beautiful are quite similar in Russian. Both names fit it well.). My favorite building in Petersburg was actually a church that was a copy of St. Basil's church in Moscow. I was rather disgusted to see that the mausoleum of Lenin (the leader of the Russian Communist Revolution) was still open and under high security. He has been pickled and on display in a coffin with a glass lid since he died in 1924. Rumor is that they close the mausoleum for 2 weeks a year to freshen him up. Other rumors are that the body parts you can see are plastic replicas. Either way, after everything that misguided guy did, he deserves to be thrown in the Moskva River. I ate at a great classic Russian Restaurant called Peter the Great. Another memorable restaurant was from the Ex-Soviet colony of Uzbekistan where we had Middle Eastern-ish food while sitting on couches around an elevated table. And the Georgian restaurants all had amazing kabobs. We also went to a Soviet bigwig cemetery. While there we saw the grave of Felix Dzerzhinsky, the founder of the KGB. Our tour guide was not amused when I said he was shit in Russian.

An interesting event happened in Moscow. It was a huge group and there were about 6 couples originally from India all traveling together. Russian food can be very bland in bad hotel restaurants especially. As the Indian diet is at least moderately spicy, they had brought little zip lock bags of mixed spices & chili powder to sprinkle over their food. I'd love to have been one of them if Russian Customs had stopped them and claimed the spices were drugs being smuggled in. I would have told the Customs officer to try snorting it to see if it was cocaine or heroin.

They all (except for my new friend-who told me the difference between travelers and tourists appropriately-who was Indian but didn't know them) **had** to go to the only Indian restaurant in Moscow. We all went to the cool amazingly good Uzbeki restaurant instead. The next day, they told us the food was horrible. Tourists ...

We went there right after an Aeroflot plane fell out of the sky, most likely due to being old and poorly maintained. While there, we missed by one day a bombing of a metro stop in Moscow. It happened just before we got on the train to go from Petersburg to Moscow.

Each trip was with a company (since bankrupted due to the Great Recession) which provided international tours for doctors and their families. They stopped at a local hospital or clinic in each big city on the itinerary so the whole trip could be used as a business travel expense. They did have the whole plan overseen by accountants and lawyers and had been doing this for over 20 years, so it was legitimate. We got a tour with a question and answer session at each place and had to write a short paper on our experience. These trips truly were a valid eye-opening thing as the practice of medicine and the places it is provided are drastically different worldwide.

The hospital visit I remember from that trip was to the world's biggest hospital, Moscow General Hospital. These hospital or clinic visits around the world tend to come in 2 types: super modern clean hi-tech hospitals in rich neighborhoods better or at least on a par with the best US hospitals or ones that look haunted, sad or like a ghetto vet's office. Moscow General shall we say is not exactly super modern. As we were walking through one of the wards, a patient on a ventilator was agitated and waving frantically to us. No staff were around to see what he wanted. I hope he just wanted to say hi … In the stairwell was a mop-bucket full of nasty water. One room had stacks of cloth mattresses full of scary looking stains. The capper to the whole visit was 2 dogs having sex on the grounds. The Soviet's badly conceived, unrealistic economic plans and heavy spending on weapons truly bankrupted the USSR. The Soviet empire had to fall.

The other clinic was not memorable in itself because the only thing I remember of it was all the TVs showing the hostage situation in southern Russia by some Chechen terrorists. It was playing non-stop while we were getting our hospital visit. They were mad after the central government completely demolished Russian Chechnya. Go figure.

My next trip was 8 years later and Putin was still there. Things had gotten better but were still not up to Western standards of infrastructure and development. One of the other doctors on the trip made the stupid mistake of drinking the hotel tap water and got the Tolstoy Trots. Her explanation was 'but it was a luxury hotel, even if the water was kinda cloudy … '. Idiot. But everyone still got the Molotov's Revenge at least once during the 2-week trip. In my book (literally), being able to drink the tap water and not get sick is the criteria for being a developed vs. a developing country,

Some of this is just that it takes quite a while to catch up. Some is that the society is still very unequal. The same former communist party hacks are still raping the country and skimming off the top of everything. Putin, the hack in chief, was KGB under the Soviets. And once you are KGB, you are always KGB. He owns all the major media to speak of. And he or his people own all the oil and gas companies. An infamous 'terrorist' attack was likely just a cover up of an evil publicity stunt in which 'terrorists' were really KGB or some such to justify whatever shenanigans Pootie & co. were up to. The lives lost in service of publicity, none of Pootie's people care I'm sure. His critics or election rivals have this nasty habit of accidentally getting polonium poisoning in London restaurants or killed by 'terrorists' in freak murders.

This time the hospital visits were not memorable and we started out in Moscow then took a long boat ride to Peter arriving there during the White Nights. Peter is so far north that in mid-summer the sun is up nearly all night long. The river trip was a great idea. We got to relax more than usual on these kinds of trips because so much time was spent getting from one place to another. And we got to see many of the smaller towns in Central Russia. One of the best things about the river cruise was getting to interact with the crew of largely recent college graduates. At a panel discussion where we got to ask them questions, I asked what they thought about the state of their government being nearly cemented into Putin's hands especially in light of the state media monopoly. They weren't optimistic to say the least. The older lady on the panel was much sunnier about the state of her country, but then she had lived through the dark days under communism. At lunch one day we sat across from one of the young girls. I asked her about whether she had read *Generation P* by the living Russian writer Victor Pelevin. In this book all the media coverage of the US and Russian presidents is pure computer-generated CGI fiction. The presidents don't even exist and nobody (among those in the know) has any clue who is really running the country. She had and loved it. Probably because it is almost true, for Russia at least. I wish Trump were a GCI fiction instead of a living fiction.

Not too long after we got back Russia got more invested in the Syrian civil war by backing Assad, the brutal dictator and their ally. If it wasn't for their backing and Putin making Assad get rid of (most) of his chemical weapons, Obama would have taken Assad out. And Islamic State would likely never have had a chance to get so big. I had read a book by Samar Yazbek, a Syrian journalist from Assad's religious sect, called *A Woman in the Crossfire*. In it she details some of the atrocities committed by Assad. As she is both a journalist and of his protected religious sect, she is pretty credible. Very hard reading. I got the bright idea of sending Putin a copy. Since he was the East German KGB chief before the fall of communism, he speaks fluent German. I went to amazon.uk (saved on shipping) and sent him a German copy to the Russian White House. His gift note read: **The author is an Alawite (Assad's religious sect) journalist. Who are you in bed with?** Ungrateful bastard never sent me a thank you note. Probably a good thing, it would have had a touch of polonium in it ...

Then he took the Ukrainian peninsula of the Crimea with its nuclear sub bases and started a civil war in the rest of Ukraine because they kicked out his stooge who was the president of the Ukraine and were making moves towards the West.

One of my favorite 'Russian' writers was actually Ukrainian, Nikolai Gogol. If you quiz most 'Russians' you meet here, most are not really Russian. Lots of Ukrainians, Armenians, Jews (never really accepted by the Russians), Belarussians, etc. He wrote one story in particular called *Taras Bulba*. In it the semi-historical title character rouses the Ukrainian Cossacks (a kind of semi-official militia) to kick out their Polish overlords. To do so he has to kill his own son who fell for a Polish girl. It is a great story in and of itself.

Of course, it made me think of my friend Pootie. This time I sent him a copy in Russian of the book it came from. This gift note said: **Re-read *Taras Bulba*. You are not a Pole. Just because your name (Vladimir) means Lord of the World, it isn't true.**

A week or two later I got an email from amazon.uk. It told me that my gift was returned so they were refunding my money, minus shipping! This means I at least got pretty close to, if not to the man himself, pissed him off **and** got my money back!

Needless to say, I will not be trying to go back to Russia while Putin is anywhere near power. Even if I could get a visa to get in the country, I don't know if I could get out alive, literally. And I plan on running any mail from Vlad under a Geiger counter ...

MY COUSIN DWAYNE WADE

Dwayne Wade: Black American professional basketball player. One of the most popular and well known.

-my definition

PCP (Phencyclidine AKA Angel Dust AKA Sherm AKA horse tranquilizer) is a weird messy drug. And so is the typical way it is smoked. Nat Sherman is a brand of those long thin dark brown things I guess would be called cigarillos. They (who knows how it got to be that brand in particular) are dipped in liquid PCP. You let them sit and dry for a few days then smoke them. Such a setup as a way to smoke PCP led to one of its nicknames, Sherm. It can also be used as a verb, Sherming. Getting high on PCP can also be called Getting Wet. It can of course be smoked like this with a regular cigarette or a joint.

The effects are also pretty messy and weird. It is both a major stimulant to the point you hallucinate and a dissociative anesthetic, meaning you still can notice pain but it doesn't bother you emotionally. Between the stimulant and hallucinations and since they can't really feel pain, people on PCP tend to get violent & be extra hard to stop because they don't respond to the pain of a takedown. And they can snap and go off unpredictably. Thanks to all that, it isn't very popular anymore except for occasional comebacks, fortunately.

During my residency, we were still seeing a lot of sherm out there & people brought to the ER after taking it. One big guy got his IV and was waiting calmly to be seen. Then something popped up in his head. He ripped out his IV and jumped onto the secretary's counter

119

with blood spraying everywhere from his IV site. Nice. Fortunately, one of the nurses' aides was a big soothing guy named Mark. Usually called Big Mark. Mark talked him down from the desk and wrapped him in a blanket in a bear hug. He mellowed and got tied to a bed until the meds to knock the drugs down worked.

Another guy got put directly into the 'safe' room tied to a bed in hard leather restraints until he got meds & mellowed. He used his free arm to pull the bed around the room to the drawer. At the time, they had scalpels in the drawer. Bad idea. He pulled one out and cut off his restraints. I looked through the little window into the room and saw his bed was empty. I opened the door and saw him in a corner holding the knife. I closed the door, locked it & let security take care of him.

Years later, PCP made a brief resurgence of popularity. The paramedics and police brought in this young black kid tripping hard on PCP. Unlike most people he seemed to be pretty happy sherming. He was laughing his ass off. I went in to see him.

He must have fixated on my name badge because I don't find it worthwhile formally introducing myself to someone who is drunk or high. He blurted out: 'Your name is Doctor Wade. Your family must have owned Dwayne Wade's family!' Unfortunately true. Also, unfortunately, all the nurses were around to hear this, one of whom was black. They all had a few laughs at my expense ...

PC NAZIS

Politically Correct: phrase. (Commonly abbreviated PC) is used to describe language, policies, or measures that are intended to avoid offense or disadvantage to members of particular groups in society.

-Wikipedia definition

Since the times keep changing it isn't the same world anymore that many people, including me, grew up in. Casually racist, homophobic or otherwise mean jokes, names or expressions used to be accepted. As society gets more aware and conscious of others feelings, it is no longer acceptable to make fun of somebody's religion, race, sexuality, disability etc. Unless you are the President of the US. Then it lets you get elected. But seriously, the Flaming Hot Cheeto in the Oval Office is a symptom of the backlash against political correctness. Many people make fun of how special and delicate 'the Lefties' are by calling them snowflakes.

But it is still not nice to call people bad names. PC is still Correct in the vast majority of cases. This is one example of how it can go too far.

The medical school used to have a tradition dating back generations called Joke Day. Anyone, student or teacher could go up on stage before a lecture and tell a joke on a Friday. As early 20s often dorky kids in a time a rapid social change aren't necessarily too PC or even aware of anything around them, some bad jokes slipped through.

The anatomy professor was the most beloved teacher at the school. He routinely won teacher of the year. And he deserved it. He told the following joke one Friday: 'This guy is waiting in a professor's office lobby for his med school acceptance interview. He sees the guy before him run out dripping sweat, puke in the trash can & run out. He is understandably worried about this & asks the guy next to him what's up? The guy tells him: 'It's ok. The professor has no ears & is really sensitive about it. Don't mention the ears & you'll be alright.' He goes in. The interview goes well & he thinks he's outta danger when the guy asks him one final question: 'Being observant is important as a doctor. I like to ask my interviewees one question to see how observant they are. What's the first thing you notice about me?' He keeps telling himself: 'Nothing about the ears. Nothing about the ears.' Then he comes out with his answer: 'You're wearing contacts!' The interviewer is flabbergasted at this. 'How could you tell that? You're the most perceptive student I have ever had. I am going to make sure you come to med school here young man! Now tell me how you could tell?' The guy answers: 'You don't have any f**king ears to hold up glasses ...'

Unfortunately, in that class was one of the people we all hated. She was older than the rest of us, always sat in the front row and always asked a lot of stupid questions that delayed the class so everyone stayed longer because of her. And apparently, she had an uncle with one freakishly small ear. She went to the Dean of the school to officially complain about the poor guy. He was forced to formally apologize in front of the whole school.

And from that day, Joke Day never happened again ...

'PERP WALKIN'

Perp Walk: phrase. Or frog march, is a practice in American law enforcement of taking an arrested suspect through a public place, creating an opportunity for the media to take photographs and video of the event.

-Wikipedia definition

The perp(-etrator) walk is a good way to inspire schadenfreude. Schadenfreude is a German word (go figure) that literally means pleasure from (others') pain. When someone gets publicly taken away to jail in front of witnesses (often holding a hand over their face), the rest of us get to see justice being done.

At my residency hospital the OB/Gyn patient rooms are in a back hall we called the 'fish tank' because of what kind of patients were seen there. Hey. I didn't come up with the name. I barely saw an attractive 20-something girl in one of the rooms as I walked by one day.

One of the surgery teams had a Physician Assistant student rotating with them. As the fish tank was also next to the trauma room, they were down there pretty regular.

The next thing I know, everyone is talking about how that guy went into the girl's room. Didn't say a word. Then promptly proceeded to do a breast exam. Then walked out. Still without saying a word. Nice. And of course, he and his team had no connection whatsoever with the patient's care.

The next and last time I saw that guy, he was on the TV news. And doing the classic hand-over-face perp walk.

Now that is some good schadenfreude … Mmm hmm, I like me some schadenfreude.

ROCKY

A small-time boxer gets a supremely rare chance to fight a heavy-weight champion in a bout in which he strives to go the distance for his self-respect.

-IMDB description of the original movie *Rocky*

I met the lady I'll call Rocky while she was smoking, drinking & using meth. Not surprisingly she looked like shit. Much older than her real age of the mid-forties. And her health was in the dumper. She had angina, heart failure and emphysema. Her boyfriend was doing the same stupid shit. He looked like Michael Keaton at the end of *Beetlejuice*, after the witch doctor shrunk his head.

I told her my standard, 'You quit all that stuff forever and get into AA to help you stay away from it or you are dead by Christmas.' She told me she hadn't even started all that until her son was killed when she was 40 and it apparently took her down internally & externally fast. Meth do that. Maybe that should be the real reason they call it speed. You speed full speed ahead into becoming a mental & physical car crash scene. We talked a little more about AA and how she can't use something bad for an excuse to kill herself moderately slowly. And that AA can help her work through her trauma and stay off the drugs. And when the boy said he was using too, I told him he had to quit & go to AA too.

Then I completely forgot about her. I have had that talk more times than I can count & usually it doesn't work.

Next time I saw her, I didn't even remember seeing her before. The nurses had written smoking/drinking/mething on the triage form like she was still using them. Among my first words to her were the standard. She told me that since she saw me a month ago, she hadn't done any of them. I congratulated her and told her sorry for not recognizing her at first.

Since she still had all the health problems, she kept coming in for shortness of breath and/or chest pain, often with a side of anxiety which makes it harder to know which was causing the problem each time. Most of the time, she still got admitted to be safe. The boy came in with her about half the time. He was supposedly sober now too. One of the times I saw her, I gave her a copy of my story, *3 of My Buddies*, about some of my male alcoholic patients, 2 of whom didn't make it out alive.

The last time I saw her, she was distraught because the boy had left her to fall off the wagon into a meth pipe. Extra hard to tell if her complaints were physical or mental. She was very depressed and crying, but still sober. I made sure she had the *3 Buddies* story still & asked her if she liked it. She had it crumpled up in her purse and liked it. We talked about how she had to take care of herself first and not let the boy ruin her sobriety and end up killing her. And keep going to AA. My gut feeling is there was no physical problem that time around but I admitted her regardless to be safe and give her a little more time off the streets to get over the boy.

There is even something called **broken heart syndrome** that she could have been having then. When somebody has a massive emotional shock, it can cause such an adrenalin surge that it stresses out the heart. They can have EKG or lab changes that look like a mild heart attack. When they do an angiogram, no clogged arteries are seen in the heart. It was discovered in Japan so has a Japanese name that means octopus bottle because the heart balloons out at the bottom like an octopus trap.

My guess is that poor Rocky didn't have broken heart syndrome in more than an emotional way. She already became the champ when she quit the smoking/drinking/mething for several months. I am in her corner.

I hope she remains undefeated but I am not overly optimistic. Even sober, she still needed to come to the ER regularly. I haven't seen her for over a year

SNAKES BITE

An old man sees a sick snake by the side of the road. He decides to be a snakeatarian and take it home. He sets it by the fireplace, feeds it and nurses it back to health. He comes home one day & the snake bites him. It's poisonous, he lives hours from a hospital, he gonna die. He asks the snake: 'Snake, WTF? I saved your life! You bit me! I'm gonna die!'

The snake turns to him and replies: 'Stupid old man. I'm a snake. What do you think I do? If you get bit by a snake and you get upset, surprised or take it personal; which is the stupider: YOU or the snake?'

-my version of a very old story that dates back at least to the *Arabian Nights*

I have always liked that story. It is super true. People do what they are capable of as a general rule. And if you get yourself upset when someone acts the way they always do; YOU are the stupid one. And everyone (besides me of course) is a snake. The only thing that differs is the specifics of their venom. I tell this story a lot. And even try to remind myself of it when appropriate. When I tell it, I normally personalize the snake's reply to cover whatever the problematic person in their life is doing that is getting them upset. If you can keep it in mind and expect people to act the way they tend to rather than be surprised and pissed off every time they do the same stupid thing, you will be happier. Not always easy to do, but better than the alternative.

I setup and ran a medical mission trip to the outskirts of Marrakech, Morocco each of the last 2 years. As this is a strictly volunteer thing, it was truly a labor of love. I really love Morocco. It is a Middle Eastern paradise in many ways. They are nearly all Muslim but of the more tolerant version thereof. The people are overall pretty happy, friendly and like tourists. Arabic hospitality is legendary. A guest is given a place of honor and plied with food. The guest bond is so strong that even an enemy is treated well as long as he is in your house. There are still camels and the other Arabic touches that exist throughout the Muslim world. The food is amazing with unique dishes and combinations of flavors not found anywhere else. They are at the Western end of the Silk Road, so have curries and spices from the East as part of their cuisine. The architecture and color schemes can be found nearly the same in Southern Spain as that used to be a Moroccan colony. This can be seen to lesser degrees even in Southern California where I live as the Spanish took it to Mexico & we stole California from them. Even the pottery has similarities to that seen in Mexico. The climate varies from the Sahara Desert to the Atlas Mountains and beaches. Several of the beatnik writers moved there at least temporarily and helped introduce the Western world to hashish which is common there. It used to be part of the hippie trail in the 60s for the surfing, the sites and the hashish. All in all, a wonderful place to visit although, as in all developing countries with a history of systematic rape & pillage by colonial powers until relatively recently, it has its challenges.

It was also a labor. Setting up an international medical mission trip remotely from the other side of the world is difficult. You need to partner with local medical schools or hospitals and get Ministry of Health permission as well as arrange translators, lodging, etc. All that eventually worked out after we took 2 trips there beforehand to meet people and make arrangements. Once it looked like it was actually going to happen, I panicked and reached out to various friends who had led similar trips. The one who came through was Adam. Adam is an incredibly cool, very impressive guy. He founded Global First Responder (globalfirstresponder.org), a non-profit that runs medical missions all over the world. We met through the International Section email list of one of the big ER doctor associations. He replied to my email & we talked. He went with us on our first meeting with the local medical school officials and eventually made our trip an official GFR trip. I couldn't have done it without him. I didn't realize it but the first year I was intended to be the official team leader and he just went along for the ride (and to make sure I was up to it). Once I realized that and felt comfortable in the role, he stuck to just seeing patients. After I took full command of the trip, I heard my name called more times than I ever have before. I was continually putting out fires and could barely see patients. Now I understand why Adam preferred to sit in the backseat for this one. Glad I could give you a vacation from leading a team, buddy! Later, he made me the official West Coast Lead Coordinator of GFR as they are in Missouri. I continue to work with them and find and run missions.

In the process I made some great friends both there and in the team I assembled from all over the world. And got pretty familiar with Morocco. One friend I met there works in a store that has all kinds of upscale souvenir items. The first time I went, we were looking at carpets. I love bargaining and my Arabic is good enough to do it mostly in that. We went through the standard negotiation process. He made a super high first offer. I then made one that was super low. He faked being ill at how shockingly low my offer was. I told him 'It's ok, I am a doctor.' I had him sit on a couch and took his pulse. My diagnosis was that he needed more charity in his heart. He laughed & said so did I. From there we settled on a mutually acceptable price. Then he made his move. He asked what I would say if he offered me 2 carpets. Without skipping a beat, I said in Arabic: 'I would say you are crazy.' He and his assistant laughed like crazy. It was a great moment. Now every time I go to Marrakech, I stop in Mustafa's store and buy something. He always gives us tea (which is actually standard if you spend any time in a store and look serious about buying). Last time we got there about lunchtime and he had the staff give us some of the food they were cooking for the employees. It was wonderful. And so is Mustafa.

One of the visits we stayed at a glamping (glamorous camping) resort. They had every outdoor activity you could think of from golf to riding jeeps, camels or horses through the desert foothills. It was a very posh place. We stayed in an adobe room the first nite. To experience all they had to offer, we stayed in a luxury tent the second. Unfortunately, it was a very hot day and the tent was exposed on a treeless rocky hill. I tried to take a nap during the day. Within minutes of laying on the pillow, my face caught on fire. Next time, if there is a next time, skipping the tent.

The first time we went with the residents from the local med school & the students acted as translators for us with the patients. Both times the patient mix was similar, poor villagers. Most of the adults were illiterate. And looked far older than their 'real' ages. But then no one really knew their ages for many. When they asked them for their age, many just brought out their ID card to show us because they didn't know & couldn't even read the card. I suspect many of the dates on those cards were guesses. The second year, we couldn't go with the residents as all the senior ones had graduated. We eventually ended up going with the interns' group and of course the same medical students. My buddy Salah, a local medical student, was THE person ultimately responsible for making the second trip possible. We kept in touch after the first trip. He and his friends got all the legwork done and all the various people together to make it possible. I appointed him the head Medical Student for the second trip. A post he filled exceptionally well. Neither of us saw very many patients that second trip since we were so busy running around taking care of whatever came up. Instead he got management and executive experience that he never would have gotten elsewhere.

One of the biggest and most popular things we were able to do was ultrasounds. While I was thinking it would be best for people with belly pain to look for gallstones, it was mostly used to do baby checks of pregnant women. Many women got to see their baby on an ultrasound for the first time. And many of the students saw their first baby ultrasound as well.

Maybe because of the poverty and generally lesser position of women in traditional societies such as an isolated Moroccan village, there were tons of people who wanted to be seen for what at bottom was anxiety and depression. They came in for all kinds of minor complaints and were patently nervous. As we didn't have the ability to hook them up with a psychologist or antidepressants for months, I spent a lot of time talking through the problems in their life and letting them know that the main problem was stress and how they reacted to it. And often told them (with the medical students) the story about the old man & the snake. Then I got into teaching them a simple meditation they could do regularly. Meditation has been proven to be about as effective as psychotherapy or medication but is free and can be done at home. I used a similar approach in Cambodia and tailored it to the Buddhism prevalent there. This time I tailored it to Islam. I had the students tell them it is **halal** (permitted in Islam) and that the Sufis (Muslim mystics) have been doing it for over 1000 years *because it works*. The students were all pretty skeptical at first, but all realized how effective it can be after seeing it work. And they will be able to offer this to patients for the rest of my career. Once I put their problems in context and gave them an easy way to fix them, almost all felt better and calmed down. One female, I wouldn't call her a lady, was sitting right behind the table where I was seeing patients. She kept butting in and trying to get ahead of other people in line. I had to tell her to wait her turn several times and to get back to her seat. I ended up taking someone behind her first and when it was her (revised) turn, I told her she got pushed back in line for being rude to her neighbors. She had all the anxiety stuff of course. She had already been seen by a cardiologist who said in the report she showed us that he recommended a psychiatrist. So of course, she came to us instead. Her hubby sounded pretty jerky and I forget what other stresses she had going on. I went through the whole spiel and told her that was exactly what the cardiologist said as well. She didn't buy it and went off in a huff. Another older lady the second year was in a full-on panic attack: hyperventilating, moaning, flopping around in a chair. Her family kept trying to 'help' by panicking as well and forcing water on her. Last I heard water doesn't fix anxiety. And just like a child having a tantrum, the more attention you give them, the worse they get. I went several times and told them to leave her alone and let her relax and her that she needed to relax and breathe normally to feel better. This didn't work so we eventually moved her to a back room and separated her from her family. Salah and I talked to her slowly and calmly for a good 45 minutes and gave her the super extended mix of this is anxiety and this is what you can do. It turned out she had already been seen for a similar episode in the local ER and told there was nothing wrong. Wrong, of course. There was something wrong in her life (I forget the specifics) and it was made worse by how she reacted to it. By the time we were done, she had calmed down and was acting normally again. I hope she took what we taught her to heart and is dealing with life more effectively still. I was rewarded a few months later when Salah messaged me about a patient he had just had. A 13-year-old girl was in the ER. The rest of his team was freaking out and trying to order all kinds of expensive, useless tests. Sal got to be a hero and fixed her problem by just sitting down and talking to her. He is a great kid and will go far someday. As will all my new friends there.

TAKE MY FLASHLIGHT ... PLEASE!

Henry 'Henny' Youngman was an English American comedian and musician famous for his mastery of the 'one-liner'; his best-known one-liner being *'Take my wife ... please'*.

-Wikipedia definition

TV doctor shows never quite get it very close to real life. Probably because real life is a lot grosser and weirder than they can put on TV.

One memorable set of patients would never be seen on TV, etc. Both happened in my internship.

The first was a very fat woman with a breathing problem. Fat and breathing problems kinda go hand in chicken grease covered hand. An early Dickens book was called *The Pickwick Papers*. The main character was obese and did this characteristic panting breathing now known medically as Pickwickian breathing. Simple math, body gets immense, lungs stay the same size. You gotta breathe faster to keep up. Not to mention the heart problems and eventual heart failure that tends to come from years of being obese. And despite the myths about smoking keeping you thin, not necessarily so. People who smoke not too likely to exercise or restrain themselves from food or drink. If you are going to do something as stupid for your health as smoking, you really think you're likely to do something hard like run or avoid something good like that 3rd cheeseburger? And of course, you will likely get emphysema if you keep smoking long enough. Anyway, this woman had been in the hospital **a few days** by the time I saw her & did a physical. As I was examining her, her 'asthma' (it's always asthma, even if you smoke for 40 years and came down with it when you were 50) inhaler fell out of a roll of fat under her breast. Since she'd been there a few days, it must have been stashed there at home & she just forgot about it. And of course, bathing or even slightly vigorous movement hadn't happened since then. Nice.

A few days later I gotta page while I was doing my ICU rotation that they had just intubated my next new patient in such and such a room and they were coming to ICU soon. I vaguely remembered the name from seeing her before. And not good memories either. I went to her room to start things because I wanted to get things outta the way to get back to sleep and not be behind if another one came soon thereafter.

When I got to the doorway of the room, I saw at least 4 nurses around an immensely fat woman lying on her back with both knees up like she was at the Gynecologist. They were trying to put a catheter in her bladder since she wasn't exactly gonna be walking to the bathroom while on a ventilator.

One nurse was on each leg holding it outta the way, another was pushing her fat floppy stomach outta the way. A fourth was holding a catheter and aiming for the hole. None of them had a flashlight so it wasn't happening. Between the sick, the poor hygiene and all those rolls of fat it smelled really nice in there.

One of the nurses asked if I had a flashlight. I did. I tossed it to her and said: 'Take my flashlight ... please!' before walking out of the room.

THE BLACK DEATH

The **Black Death**, also known as the **Great Plague** or the **Plague**, or less commonly the **Black Plague**, was one of the most devastating pandemics in human history, resulting in the deaths of an estimated 75 to 200 million people in Eurasia and peaking in Europe from 1347 to 1351.

-Wikipedia definition

The plague has been a huge thing in my life. My third year of college I was still pre-veterinary but starting to be ready to change. I was working for a vet and he wasn't terribly happy seeming at his job. And from what I could see it wasn't terribly happiness inducing. People call pediatrics and geriatrics veterinary medicine. Your patients at either extreme of the lifespan are not able to talk to you and tell you what is wrong, nor understand why you are hurting them. And worse they can have parents/adult children/owners who can be at either extreme: overly helicopter-y and in your face about everything or abusive/neglectful assholes. Pretty good argument against veterinary medicine, peds or geriatrics in my book (literally in my book). And I had just finished a test in my agribusiness/pre-vet major. The test question was: 'You have just inherited a large quantity of $. You decide to use this $ to open a pig farm (EXACTLY what I would do conveniently enough). Please describe in detail how you would setup the farm with room for breeding, food storage, waste disposal, etc. Nice.

Then I had my first microbiology class. The teacher read a case report from the Centers for Disease Control's Morbidity & Mortality

Weekly Report (CDC MMWR), a sampling of trending infection or toxic events. The case he read was about a case of modern-day plague. It still exists today but as people became more used to it after the Black Death & just peoples' and bacterial evolution, it is rare and almost only associated with desert rodent exposure anymore.

He described how the bacteria literally fill the blood vessels with bacteria. And how from getting sick to dying can be as fast as a day or less. And how they can get the black swollen lymph nodes in the groin & armpits called buboes. This is where the terms Black Death and Bubonic Plague come from. He also talked about how sometimes it can spread to the lungs and become much more easily spread by coughing instead of requiring rat fleas the normal way.

This came at THE right time for me. That day I decided to change my major to microbiology and my goal to med school. And I made the right choice. People are much better conversationalists and by virtue of that much more interesting to work with than animals. And as long as you see non-demented/drunk/high adults or older children, you don't have to torture things that don't at least understand the reason for the torture. And the adult children/parents/owners issue doesn't come up.

Since then I have had an interest in the plague. It literally changed the face of Europe. Before the Black Death, Europe was feudal, where the majority of people were essentially the property of the local lord. The tremendous social change initiated by the plague (and other historical trends at the same time) got rid of the feudal system in all but Russia within a 100 years or so. This freeing of the individuals to live where and how they wanted and general mobilization of society was one of the biggest contributors to the Renaissance and modernity in general.

I have found and read several books that deal with the plague since then. One of the best is by the French Nobel winner Camus and called *The Plague*. It describes a fictionalized version of one of the last modern widespread outbreaks of the plague in North Africa, where Camus was born and grew up. It is a riveting account that includes all the standard stuff you see in an outbreak: dead rats, buboes, mass graves. But Camus was an Existentialist, meaning he was interested in how people should act in a world where there is not necessarily a God. So, the book is also about more than just the rats, it focuses on a group of accidental friends who band together to deal with the situation. And everyone has a crisis of conscience, even the priest. Quite a great book, one of my all-time favorites.

Another is *A Journal of the Plague Year* by Daniel DeFoe, the writer of *Robinson Crusoe*. It is about the 1666 London Plague. He was born not long after the Plague, so was able to draw on survivors and recent records. It is a purely journalistic account of the Plague and gets into the reactions to and management of this overwhelming event. Nice book if you are interested in the Plague.

Much later, I found out that Oxford University has summer school for adults who can afford to study in Oxford. We made plans to do that a few years ago after visiting Oxford. When we looked online at the available courses, the one that jumped out at me was called *The Plague*. Of course, I took that one. I brought a fake concert T-shirt that I have had for years. It looks like your standard black long-sleeved concert shirt. Except on the front it has a picture of a rat surrounded by flies and 'Black Death European Tour 1347-51.' The back has the 'concert' locations. While there we learned tons about the Plague and its societal aftereffects. As this was right after the big Ebola outbreak, it was even more topical. ANY disease, from Ebola to the Plague or even the common flu can mutate overnite and turn drastically more severe and/or more contagious.

We live in a world where when, not if, the next big epidemic comes up; it will be spread worldwide within days.

Get your flu and other shots.

And be afraid. Be not so very afraid ...

THE BLOOD OF JESUS

And he took the cup, and gave thanks, and gave *it* to them, saying, Drink ye all of it; For this is my blood of the new testament, which is shed for many for the remission of sins.

-Jesus, Matthew 26:27-28

My last rotation in med school was in the psych ER. This was at the County hospital in LA right after the latest big earthquake took out the psych building there. Since the old hospital was the 2nd biggest in the world they found temporary places for the psych patients. When I first started med school in '91, they told us: 'by the time you graduate, the new hospital will be open.' Not so much. The earthquake relief funds gave them something like $200 million extra for rebuilding. Even with the extra $ it wasn't open until 2007. And conveniently for the county budget but not for every private ER in the county, it went from about 800 beds to 220 or so. This meant they are always overcapacity & uncompensated patients go to the next local ER &/ or hospital which get 15% of what they bill from the lawsuit lost by the greedy lying bastards at the tobacco companies as part of a legal settlement. Again, not surprisingly, many local private hospitals went belly up about then. And the scandal resulted in the TV show *Code Black* about how overfull the hospital was at all times.

The temporary psych screening area was a little room of cubicles where they saw you and decided if you got put on a California legal code section 5150 3 day psychiatric hold until they could medicate you or get more time through the courts to get you safe to be out on the streets again. One day, everyone was talking about this woman who smelled BAD. They put her on a 5150 hold and sent her to the medical side of the ER to find out about the stank. Someone wasn't keeping their eye on the smelly ball and she eloped between the 2 places. Of course, the county hospital is close to skid row, so she was brought back in a few days later. The first question they asked her was: 'So babe, what's the stink?' her answer was: 'My menstrual blood is the blood of Jesus, and you wouldn't want that to go to waste, now would you?' She was the Roach Motel of tampons. Tampons went in, they never came out. Nice.

They made the mistake of talking to the legal idiots who said: 'She doesn't have a fever, she doesn't have a high white blood cell count (indicating infection), she's not in septic shock YET; so we can't violate her civil rights by forcing those out of her.' Extra nice.

The temporary holding area at the time for 5150 patients waiting to get placed into a more long-term psych hospital was a C-shaped room barely bigger than many peoples' living room. If you were in need of restraints, they had chairs bolted to the floor and shackles built into the armrests.

For her entire time there, anyone who wasn't tied to a chair frothing at the mouth was on the opposite side of the C from her at all times. I came in one morning after she'd had a few days of psych meds. She told me: 'Gimme a sandwich.' So I told her: 'OK but first you gotta get in the bathroom and take those things out.' She went in and closed the door.

There was less than ½ inch of a gap under the door, but it got pretty thick in there pretty fast. When I looked out the window birds were falling out of the sky and the sun got noticeably dim. Even nicer.

After she was in there about 5 minutes, someone said we should open the door to make sure she wasn't doing a Robin Williams. When we opened the door there were 6-8 coal black tampons in a pile on the floor.

The Blood of Jesus was mighty stanky that day my friends.

The epilogue may or may not have been the same woman. The ages, schizophrenia and coochie fixation would fit. But I can't even guess about the name of the Roach Motel. I do remember 'Julie.' She was in her late 30s and for several months would come in saying she was 7 months pregnant. She of course was not. It was all her schizophrenia. Of course, she never took her meds. When you told her, she was not pregnant she didn't believe you and got belligerent. One time she was taking to jail and temporarily barred from the ER for attacking a coke machine in the lobby after getting in an argument with it.

I have spent too much of my time over multiple visits telling her: 'No you are not pregnant. That is you're schizophrenia talking.' An old friend loves to tell people how that was one of the first things he knew about me from overhearing it when he came in to see a patient. Of course, he tells it out of context to make it funnier.

One time she came in and one of the nurses recognized her from high school. Apparently, her dad was an abusive drunk. Schizophrenia is largely genetic but a bad environment can make it more likely or worse. Looks like her dad screwed her by giving her his genes & environment. She was always reasonably well dressed for a schizophrenic and the nurses said an older guy would sometimes come in and give her cash. Looks like dad was trying to make up for his past behavior. I REALLY hope it wasn't some sugar daddy with a fetish for crazy chicks …

THE BUBBLE

Retinal detachment is a disorder of the eye in which the retina separates from the layer underneath. Symptoms include an increase in the number of floaters, flashes of light, and worsening of the outer part of the visual field. This may be described as a curtain over part of the field of vision. In about 7% of cases both eyes are affected. Without treatment permanent loss of vision may occur.

-Wikipedia definition

I started to notice problems seeing about the time I hit 40. I was having problems seeing the eardrum with the otoscope. There was a Bruce Willis sci-fi movie called *The Surrogate*. The billboards had the title and a pic of Brucie with a hot girl. The hot girl was a cyborg from the waist down. Despite driving past the ad for weeks, I never figured the waist down part out until much later. I thought it was some kinda sexy romancey thing.

Turned out I had cataracts both eyes. Likely from growing up in Arizona and rarely wearing sunglasses. Maybe some from not running and hiding like a cockroach when they shot X-rays in the ER. Freakishly young regardless. I had to get surgery on each eye to take out the old lens and put in a plastic one. Fun.

As part of the workup before surgery, they checked my retinas by dilating my eyes. It got even better. Because I have read a lot my whole life, my eyes have stretched (a big reason people need to wear glasses for far vision). This meant the retinas had stretched and thinned out as well. With all the pulling and tugging on the eye during cataract surgery, there is a 1% chance each eye that you will get a torn retina. Mine, because of the thin retinas, was 2% each. Still, pretty good odds & the surgery needed to be done regardless. But I got shitty luck. More on that next.

I had the first eye done and except for it hurting like a mother ... it all seemed to go well. Then while I was visiting my parents in Arizona, we went out for dinner the nite before I was going back home. I saw out of that eye this weird bright green slow-moving line at the edge of my vision. Looked kinda like a lightning bolt. It went away before we got to the restaurant so I thought it might just be a (harmless) side effect of the surgery. Next day at lunch I had my glasses hooked onto the collar of my shirt. Again, I saw something outta that eye off to the side. I thought it was the glasses slipping off & that I was seeing the earpiece pop up. Not so lucky. The glasses were in place. **My retina wasn't**. Shortly afterward I started seeing tons of little floating things in that eye about the size of near transparent grains of sand (individual retinal cells) and big irregular dark chunks (pieces of retina). Since the retina is like the photo sensor in a digital camera that converts light into info the brain can use, it is kinda nice to have in place. It is a big emergency, because if it comes off the back of the eye entirely, it can rarely be put back in place and work very well thereafter.

I called the retina eye doctor I had seen before the surgery for a consult. Fortunately, I worked with his wife who is an ER doc also & they are both cool people. He sent me to a retina specialist in Phoenix. The guy confirmed what I already knew.

The retina is very thin & fragile so you can't actually touch it; much less sew it back in place. It's like very thin wet toilet paper. The main treatment is using a laser to burn it at the edge and that makes a scar which holds it down. Unfortunately, the scarring process takes about 2 weeks once the laser is done, so it is still high risk to get worse for a while. Burning the inside of your eye with a laser sounds fun, doesn't it? Surprisingly it's not. Each laser burn feels like you are being punched in the eye. And they potentially need to do dozens to build a firewall around a tear. After the first couple laser jabs, I asked for something for the pain. He put in drops (good) then did a novocaine-y dentist-y type shot onto the surface of the eyeball itself (actually not as bad as it sounds, but that's not saying much, is it?) then finished his lasering.

I flew home that nite and went straight to Raghu (the retina guy). He said the guy wasn't very good and hadn't properly positioned the eye, so the laser burns weren't in the right place to do their job. This time I got a different treatment. Frostbite/cold burn by applying Q-tips soaked in liquid nitrogen to the outside of the eye. Again, not fun, but Raghu is hyper-competent, so he numbed it up again *beforehand*. By this point, a needle in the eye was nothing. It has the side effect of giving you the worst red eye ever and making the surface of the eye swell. Looks real pretty.

I had to work the next nite. I went in but within about 20 minutes, I had to tap out and go home because there were so many retinal chunks floating around it was hard to see. I would see things appear outta the corner of my eye that looked like a cat or rat running past at first. And there was also the risk that if I had to lift or strain, that might cause pressure changes in my eye that would make the tear worse.

I called Raghu & we made plans for surgery the next day to do a more definitive fix. I went into the surgery thinking he would clean things up in there and do lasering from inside and I'd be good. Not so much. Again, I got shitty luck. When I woke up from surgery I was face down. Raghu told me things were worse than he expected. He did the cleanup & the lasering, but then filled my eye with gas to act as scaffolding to hold the retina in place until it had a chance to scar down. It slowly gets absorbed over a week and a half or so, by which time it has hopefully done its job.

The problem comes from this thing they call **gravity**. Gas rises as a general rule. The retina is at the back of the eye. This means that for the bubble to actually work as a scaffold, I had to keep my head/face down constantly. Super nice. I was allowed *5 minutes a day of face up time*. Sleeping on a hemorrhoid pillow. Which normally meant not sleeping much at all and then waking up, realizing I was on my side & going back to the torture pillow. They actually rent special chairs with a round hole facing down over an attached table to rest your neck. It allows you to eat and has a special mirror built into it so you can watch TV. Try bending your neck straight down and holding it there for 5 minutes or so. Neck feels pretty bad, pretty fast, no? Imagine how it felt after over a week of this. Things went off ok after the bubble went away.

A few months later I started to have worse vision on that side and it ended up being from cloudiness of the thin layer of cells at the back of the lens. A common, pretty harmless side effect of the cataract surgery. A quick painless laser job and that was over.

Then it was time for the second lens. Since there was so much pain from the first surgery and later the torn retina, the cataract surgeon decided to put all the nerves in my eye socket to sleep for the surgery. That way, it wouldn't move during the surgery, hopefully reducing the postop pain & lowering the chance of a tear. It went well with no short-term problems. At least if you don't count the double vision I had from the 2 eyes not moving together for a few minutes after I woke up.

Then several months later, we moved. I was lifting, etc. during the move. And later at work, I had to sew up a guy's cut finger. Seemed like a cool, reasonable guy. He was somewhere in his mid-forties but still smoked, so by definition not a full adult in my book until proven otherwise. He proved NOT. As I was injecting the novocaine-y stuff into his finger, he started kicking his little feet into the air like a 5-year-old would in similar circumstances. Unfortunately, he was not 5, so nobody was holding him down. One of his knees connected to my forehead. Normally nothing, barely felt it. But then I saw this shower of fine sandy stuff in the recently operated eye. I at first thought it was flecks of dried blood from his finger being dispersed into the air as I started to put away the stuff from the sewing job. Not so much. Torn retina in the 'good' eye.

This one ended up being much worse of a tear. Straight to surgery. Back into the bubble torture chamber. This time, from the start I had what I at first thought were floaters stuck to the back of the new lens. Right in the middle of my vision on the now bad eye were what looked like 3 or 4 little pieces of rat feces. I went to the cataract doctor and he said no. Raghu saw me and gave me the bad news. Apparently, some of the liquid in the eye had slipped under the tear and separated the retina from the back of the eye. The retina was dead there. Right in the middle of my visual field. Nice.

But as the eye healed it got to the point where I no longer saw the dead spot on a day to day basis. I still see it when I have the good eye closed and am looking at an eye chart in a dark room. But I can cheat and move my eye around to see everything by using the good part of the retina. And I still see it through my closed lids if I am looking at a bright light. Or sometimes at night when I close my eyes, I see a negative, glowing afterimage of it. It has gotten slowly smaller over the years but is still there. Like God in the Old Testament leading the Hebrews out of Egypt: a pillar of smoke by day, a pillar of fire by nite.

When my eyes are both open in normal lighting, I don't even notice it at all. With normal light and only the bad eye open, I don't see the spot, but the vision isn't that good either.

Vision only starts in the eye. It goes from there to the brain. The brain has different layers of complexity for putting vision info into stuff we actually 'see'. It also uses the largely overlapping (except at the outer edges) info from both eyes to make 1 single image. My brain is constantly lying to me and making sh*t up to fill in that blank spot.

Kinda cool, and definitely very weird. But then so is the brain
And mine weirder than others. Ask people who know me.
I doubt you're gonna find any who disagree ...

THE DUCK HUNTING JOKE

This is an old joke, but I like my version the best. I have heard it all over, even once in India. That guy left off the psychiatrist though. It makes fun of all the major specialties & their quirks.

5 or 6 docs decide to go hunting ducks. They decide to take turns.

First up is the Internal Medicine doc. These guys have the nickname of fleas. Just like fleas, they hover around peoples' bodies sucking blood. And they are the last specialist to leave a corpse. They supposedly prefer to wear their stethoscopes wrapped around their necks like a scarf. For this reason, that style of stethoscope wearing is called a 'flea collar'.

That guy hears wings, jumps up, aims and says:

'Duck!

Wait!

Can't rule out mallard, can't rule out grebe … Need full blood chemistry test, complete blood cell count, 24-hour urine collection, ferritin level, porphyrinobilinogen level, bone marrow biopsy, CAT scan, MRI, ultrasound. Consult my friend the cardiologist, that guy will give me $50. I like that guy. Too bad he can't do medicine for s**t. Consult my other friend the kidney doctor. Wait, I'm a kidney doctor. F*** it, that guy will give me $35! Consult my other friend the dermatologist. Cheap pimple popping bastard! He'll only give me $10. But hey, $10 is still $10.

Wait! Where'd the thing go?'

Next up is the Radiologist. These guys are commitment phobic. Never marry a radiologist. They can never just say what the X-ray has, they always have to hedge their bets. For this reason, the official plant of the Radiological Society of America is the hedge.

That guy hears wings, jumps up, aims and says:

'Duck!

Wait!

Can't rule out robin red breast, consistent with partridge. Need more information from referring gamekeeper. Need clinical correlation. Request additional views. Request AM CAT scan, MRI and ultrasound.

Wait! Where'd the thing go?'

Next up is the Psychiatrist.

That guy hears wings, jumps up, aims and says:

'Duck!

Wait!

Maybe it wanted to be a swan when it grew up. Maybe its parents pressured it into becoming a duck. Maybe it has an Oedipal complex …

Wait! Where'd the thing go?'

Next up is the Surgeon. These guys choose to go into a specialty where 90% of their patient interactions involve people who are knocked out. For some reason this doesn't bode well for their people skills.

That guy hears wings, jumps up, aims, shoots and brings it down.

He turns to the pathologist and says:

'You! That's right, You! You f***ing lab rat mother-f***er! Go tell me what that f***ing thing is! And if you're wrong, I'm gonna kick your mother-f***ing teeth down your mother-f***ing throat! Why are you still standing there!?!'

The last guy up is the ER doc. Way too many of my colleagues order every test on every patient because they don't have a clue what's going on &/or the courage in their convictions to live without un-needed tests. They are a big part of why American medicine is the most expensive and far from the best in the world. I dread following these clowns because they can't make a decision to save their lives (much less that of a patient's or the Medicare trust fund), so it is always a full ER and lobby when I come in after them.

That guy hears wings, jumps up, pulls out an AK-47 and doesn't stop shooting for about 20 minutes. Brings down a low flying airplane, brings down everything in the 3 surrounding counties.

Then he says:

'What was that?'

THE GOONIES

In order to save their home from foreclosure, a group of misfits set out to find a pirate's ancient valuable treasure.

-IMDB description of the movie *The Goonies*.

For my psych rotation in medical school, I opted for C & L (Consult and Liaison). This meant I would see patients who were admitted for medical problems that had psychiatric issues as well. Much better than the Land of the Living Dead that is your typical psych inpatient ward. My most memorable patient from the entire month was a guy with schizophrenia and a big beer (or whatever) belly who showed up at the ER with his luggage because he was losing weight. The Suitcase Sign is **always** a bad sign when you see someone coming into the ER. This means that the patient has already decided they **are** going to be admitted. Often this is because they are homeless and want 3 meals a day, a warm bed and a shower. Granted there are some people with serious conditions who know they will need to stay and choose to be smart about things. I personally wouldn't go to the ER for anything without bringing a book and maybe a backpack for water, snacks, etc. But, the vast majority of the time it doesn't bode well.

Keep in mind the guy had a big belly, but he somehow talked both the ER doc and the Internal Medicine doc into admitting him to rule things like cancer, TB, hyperthyroid, etc. Neither of those guys spent enough time talking to him to find out what was really going on.

That's where I came in. It turns out the guy lives in a board and care (B & C) because he can't function well enough to take care of himself. I asked him what's going on and he told me this story. The Devil and his henchmen, the Goonies were spying on him, of course. They had inserted a listening device in his ear to find out what he was saying (Why wouldn't they?). His similarly mentally ill roommate in the B&C was also in on the plot, Duh. I of course nodded along with that stuff as it is the typical kind of classic paranoid delusions seen in schizophrenia.

Then I asked what that had to do with him losing weight. That's when it went from typical crazy to bat-shit crazy. When everybody else at the B & C was asleep, the Devil & the Goonies would put a **female** shoe on his penis and use that to suck out his blood and semen. That of course was why he was losing so much weight, Double Duh.

Schizophrenics have something called negative symptoms which include poverty of affect (limited external emotions), flat affect (similar, meaning they don't get excited/upset) and poverty of thought (not much going on upstairs). These are contrasted with positive symptoms like delusions, hallucinations (almost always auditory, not visual despite what they showed in *A Beautiful Mind*) and paranoia.

As the guy was telling me this story, that if it were happening to you or me, would have us pretty upset to say the least, his voice was a monotone and he showed less emotion than R2D2 from the *Star Wars* movies.

At one point, I was considering maybe even going into psychiatry because it is (or can be) fascinating where the mind goes. Then I realized that at best, like my patient, when they are living in a controlled environment where they get their psych meds on a regular basis, they are still grievously affected. The meds don't work that well. They don't like the sedation &/or weight gain that comes with them or the voices start telling them that the meds are poison or alien listening devices so they stop taking them.

Even worse, the lack of anything like what we would consider normal emotions or reactions caused by the negative symptoms robs these people of a crucial part of being human. If I wanted to work with that kind of patient, I would have went to vet school like my original plan. But then Fluffy would have shown more emotion when I was seeing her than your typical schizophrenic ...

THE GYPSY COOCHIE CURSE

'People are always telling me to get a job, get married, get a life, have kids, make something of myself, buy a house, be responsible, get a mortgage, get a bank account; I say: F**k That. It's so much easier doing heroin ...'

-my paraphrase of the opening lines of the movie *Trainspotting*.

The Gypsy people are a quite different subculture wherever they settle worldwide. The name is because they were thought to come from E**gyp**t. It is also the source of the term **gyp**ped, as in conned (in theory by gypsies). More on that later. Actually, they are from Western India. Their name for themselves is the Rom (pronounced like the city in Italy) or the Roma. In their language it means 'man'. In Europe this is the most common name for them. This adds to the confusion as they are most prevalent in Eastern Europe and people assume it means they are Romanian. Due to the prejudice against them they tend to say they are from Eastern Europe as well.

They tend to keep to their own community and don't truly trust outsiders. Same applies to marriages, which often happen at what most of us would consider very young ages, often to relatively close relatives. They tend to be semi-nomadic, often to stay off the grid. As best as I can understand it their worldview is that all the non-gypsies out there are chumps for working so hard. If they can get by on public assistance and various scams like fortune telling or reselling flowers outside a store at a high mark up, then they win while the rest of us are working forty hours a week and sending our kids to school. In Europe (where it seems easier to game the system), they are known for claiming more kids for public assistance than they actually have.

Apparently, in the gypsy language the English words 'God Bless You' sound similar to their words for 'F**k You'. I have been blessed several times. So far, I have resisted the temptation to bless anyone back ...

Please don't think I am a racist. I am trying to report as impartially as I can what really happens. I don't see colors. The only reason I know I am white is that the cops don't shoot me when they pull me over for speeding.

Among other things, the gypsies are famous for and have been hugely influential with their music. This may be because it comes at least partially from India which has a radically different style of music and even different musical scales from standard Western music. Their music has influenced Western classical and modern music from Liszt and Brahms in classical to jazz through Django Reinhardt to Spanish flamenco.

In the ERs, they are infamous for drug seeking, often coming in several at a time to get pain or anxiety meds in the ER and a nice Rx as a door prize. They are often demanding and rude if they don't get what they want. They also request only the narcotics that get them more mentally high than the rest and of course are 'allergic' to everything else. 'Oh, and by the way doc, I'm special, I need twice the normal maximum dose of the narcotics to control **my** pain.' Any seasoned ER worker can spot them a mile away. As there is a very small breeding pool, the faces tend to look pretty similar. Between the accent and the fact that most of them smoke 10 packs a day, the voice is a dead giveaway as well. And, not coincidentally 90% of drug addicts smoke. And of course, they all get the Marlboro face starting about 19 years old. And the names are usually patently fake. Never Indian sounding. Rarely even Eastern European. Often adjectives like Quick. Really? Really? If you're going to use a fake name, at least go to the effort to make it sound halfway real. I guess skipping out on public schooling isn't the best idea …

One particular gypsy 'lady' would come in regularly. And I have a high bar for giving someone the name lady (or gentleman for that matter) the definition of lady requires a minimum level of bearing and behavior. Just because you have a vagina, does not make you a lady. Nor does possession of a penis make you a gentleman. A more appropriate term is female or woman or male or man (although again just having a penis does not make you a man) or guy. A pet peeve of mine is when the paramedics bring in a drunk covered in some combination of his own vomit, urine or feces and say: 'This gentleman … '. Even if he was dressed like Mr. Peanut in a top hat, bowtie, cane & monocle that is a **guy**, not a **gentleman**.

Anyway, this gypsy **female** had Lupus which can cause bone and joint pain among many other things. Hers tended to be in the chest/ribs/breastbone (assuming it all wasn't just a ploy for pain meds). Since she was 50ish and Lupus potentially can make you more likely to get heart attacks, etc. she always got labs and an EKG. If those came back normal, I had a talk about how it still could be a heart problem, but was most likely just the Lupus. The first time I saw her, I gave her a Rx of some steroids to mellow that out and told her to take tylenol and motrin for the pain & see her MD in the morning.

She ripped up the steroid Rx (because she wanted narcotics), cursed out all of the staff (including me of course) and stormed out. As Lupus is a chronic condition, just like desire for Vicodin, she kept coming back. Every time I saw her face, my face fell in disappointment. She noticed this. The last time I saw her she brought her sister and I overheard her telling the sister 'He doesn't like me. I think he's prejudiced'. When I went to see her, one of the first things I said was: 'Do you remember the first time you saw me?' and I asked if the sister was there that time, she wasn't. Then I reminded her of how she acted that first time. And told her: 'Now why would you think I would be less than happy to see you?' her sister was on my side and told her so. And she actually apologized.

155

Another gypsy **guy** I only saw once, fortunately. He had lost a leg years before. And had the habit of putting rubbing alcohol on it while smoking. Don't hate. How dare you assume it was not smart to do something like smoke while putting something highly flammable on your body. That's how he rolls. And don't you dare suggest he quit smoking. You hater, you. But anyway, it caught fire. He had the equivalent of a mild sunburn on the leg. I had the nurses put some cream on it & give him a tylenol with codeine and sent him home. But he of course wanted some entirely inappropriate Vicodin to go home with. Not happening. After I told him so, there was a Code Blue upstairs I had to go take care of. As I was coming back to the ER, he was in the hallway and started chasing me around in a wheelchair harassing me for a script. I had security show him the door.

When's the last time your job included being chased down the hall by a one-legged gypsy while being shaken down for narcotics? Think of that next time you complain about your doctor bill.

Another memorable set is the mother & daughter tag-team I'll call Violet and Patty. And I do mean tag-team. If they come in together, they co-operate to make it more likely at least one will get the golden shot. Both smoke like crazy of course. Mom is late 50s, so if she comes in for chest pain, between the Marlboro & the age, she has to stay to make sure it's not a heart attack. The nurses know her enough to tell her: 'If you say it's chest pain, the doctor is going to want to admit you. Are you sure it's chest pain?' At which point it suddenly becomes back pain, conveniently enough. She of course 'requires' double the max dose of the narcotic that gives you the best mental high for **her** back pain, as she is glad to tell you. If she comes in solo, her daughter sometimes calls to remind you of that 'fact'. Of course, it is sheer stupidity to give anyone a narcotic shot for anybody's chronic pain **ever**. It only lasts a few hours. Are they going to call 911 every 3 hours for the rest of their life? Unfortunately, some do. Her favorite MO is to call 911 and come in moaning like some kind of sea monster. Then she continually leaves her room and walks to the nurses' station. She stands with her head a little down and her long hair dangling and commences the moaning. She looks like the evil girl ghost from the movie *The Ring* all grown up after smoking like crazy for years. But scarier. And no wet spot or snail trail besides Eau d'Marlboro. She knows if she is irritating enough, she might get something just to shut her up.

The daughter is bipolar and of course 'needs' narcotics for her chronic back pain. And is 'allergic' to the most common antipsychotic given in the ER. This medicine can cause muscle spasms **if** you don't give it with a benadryl chaser. It is a side effect, not an allergy. Regardless, many schizophrenics are 'allergic' to it because there are too many stupid docs out there who don't give it with the benadryl. Are there any bartenders out there so dumb they don't at least offer salt & lime with your tequila shot? Of course, she doesn't take or even fill the Rx for her psych meds. She never forgets her Marlboro Rx, conveniently enough. Sometimes she pulls the suicidal card because she knows if she is there waiting for hours or days to get into a psych hospital, she will definitely get something to shut her up and get her high.

Her latest con is rather tricky. One of the new antipsychotics is now reportedly being abused to get high. It is a downer & as a I mentioned elsewhere; some people are cheap dates who will take anything to get a little high. Not to mention, the abuse of this med is new, so many if not most docs out there don't realize why it is being requested by name like my little friend Patty does. I would be surprised if the real reason she has run out of her Rx every time you see her is that the family sit around popping her pills when they are bored. And they seem to have a low threshold for boredom. She also uses the Moaning in Your Face Technique she learned from mom to get something to shut her up. One time that I saw her, she laid down in the street and started moaning. An innocent bystander stopped her car to see what was wrong. Big mistake. Patty hopped in the passenger seat and didn't leave it until the paramedics called by the Good Sucker-amaritan showed up to bring her to the ER.

So anyway, one of the local gypsy families had the name the 'Munsters'. And boy, were they ookier and spookier than the TV version. One day one of the wives came in because her husband cheated on her with her sister. And the sister gave the husband gonorrhea. And the husband gave it to my patient. Nice.

As I was doing the exam and getting swabs from her vagina to send to the lab, one drop of the coochie juice went flying. It landed on my wrist, just past the cuff of the rubber glove. Extra nice.

Eventually I was able to wipe that from my memory banks. But then I fell snowboarding less than 6 months later. Broken right where the coochie juice landed on my dominant hand. Got surgery and pins in my wrist for a month. And couldn't work. Super nice.

Less than 6 months later we were visiting some friends who lived on the central coast. They talked me into riding ATVs on the sand dunes because even though I didn't want to, I didn't want to be a party pooper. Went up a dune too fast, the backside of the dune dropped off suddenly and I went over the handlebars landing on the same wrist. Broke, surgery, pins, no work for a month, AGAIN. Super creepy by now.

While I am a pure atheist and believe in no supernatural things of any kind, I do believe in the Gypsy Coochie Curse …

THE LAST ARAB WINTER

Tarek el-Tayeb Mohamed Bouazizi (29 March 1984 – 4 January 2011) was a Tunisian street vendor who set himself on fire on 17 December 2010, which became a catalyst for the Tunisian Revolution and the wider Arab Spring against autocratic regimes. His self-immolation was in response to the confiscation of his wares and the harassment and humiliation inflicted on him by a municipal official and her aides.

-Wikipedia definition

I was in Egypt the year before the start of the Arab Spring. Egypt is of course a tourist hot spot. At every tourist site we went, even at the rock quarry where they got some of the stones for various monuments when it was 104 degrees, there were tons of tourists. You had to go in groups through most of the sites because there were so many people that you could barely get around them. You would think that with all this tourist money, Egypt would be rich. Think again. It is one of the more economically challenged places in the Middle East. It is overpopulated and essentially the only habitable places outside the coasts are stuck along the Nile River. I lay the blame however on one man, Mubarak. It was impossible to not know who the president was in Egypt. His picture (probably about 20 or more years younger and more handsome/forceful than he looks anymore) was EVERYWHERE. Signs, billboards, TV, you name it his picture was on it. Mubarak was your typical post-colonial President for Life.

He had been in power for at least 20 or 30 years. He was famously corrupt as was his family. There has never been for more a few years a good, modern leader of Egypt. Many Egyptians think that the people can't be trusted with electing a normal ruler & say: 'Egypt needs a Pharaoh.' Mubarak maintained order by torturing & imprisoning anybody who threatened his rule, including the (non-terrorist group) the Muslim Brotherhood, that were trying to get political change.

During a previous trip to Turkey, the leader on a billboard thing was repeated exactly the same as in Egypt, with one big difference. Here the leader was Ataturk (father of the Turks) who founded modern secular Turkey about 100 years before. Kind of like having George Washington's picture hit you in the face 30 or 40 times just going to the store and back. Turkey at the time had a government that was so secular, that they were overly harsh to observant Muslims. Women were forbidden to wear the head scarf in public universities. This is rather extreme when you consider Turkey is over 95% Muslim. Since then a religious party has taken over and now things are way on the side of being too intolerant to the secular Muslims. I haven't spent much time in Turkey since then, but can almost guarantee Ataturk is a lot harder to find now that the government is trying to reverse the secular shift he started.

Morocco was between the two, both in timing of the trips and overall atmosphere. The king was everywhere, just like Mubarak or Ataturk. But (this) king is popular and genuinely seems to be trying to do the best for his country. There was no religious (or secular) discrimination. Like most post-colonial countries, Morocco is poor, but nowhere near as bad as in Egypt. Maybe it is just me, but it seems like the king's pictures were put-up all-over Morocco more out of true affection for a good ruler than shoved down people's throats as a way of backing the current regime.

Right before the Arab Spring, we were in Sub-Saharan Africa doing the typical safari thing in Kenya & Tanzania. Fun and amazing places in and of themselves but separated from the Arab World by the Sahara Desert so quite different cultures and people.

While there, I read the *International New York Times* whenever I could find it. I happened to get to read one shortly after Mohamed Bouazizi set himself on fire. I remember vividly while I was reading it that the columnist said: 'Remember this story. This guy will become famous. He will change the world.'

From there we flew out through Dubai & stayed there an extra day to see this Arabic 'Vegas'. Unfortunately, it ended up being too much like the Western Vegas. While the tallest building in the world was neat, it was 80% unoccupied due to the Great Recession that had started right as it was finishing up. And they weren't setup at the time for visitors to ride the elevator to the top for the view like at the Empire State Building. And there are many other incredibly artistic new buildings there as well. Giant aquariums where you can pay to swim with dolphins, a mall full of luxury brands and an indoor ski/snowboard hill, a resort built on artificial islands shaped like a palm tree. The things that were missing were people. Due to the recession, much of this artificial playhouse was empty. And the people that regular visitors saw were all foreign laborers. Tons of Indians, Filipinos and even an Afghan, but no natives. On a much later trip, I had a long layover in the airport at Qatar. It was the same: expensive name brands and cheap foreign labor. Apparently, all the rich oil monarchies have the same feel. Not worth visiting a place where you are only able to interact with immigrant labor in my book.

That reporter was right however. After Bouazizi died, antigovernment rallies and riots spread throughout much of the Arabic world. The Tunisian president ended up resigning. Libya descended into Hell on Earth after Obama tried to help the 'right' side in their civil war. Bahrain's Shiite Muslim majority lost even more rights after their neighbor Saudi Arabia propped up the Sunni minority sheik. Morocco had demonstrations as well. Characteristically the king handled it well. He listened and gradually reformed the government to be more representative and fair. He is still there and still loved. Mubarak acted like Mubarak. He fought and held onto power as long as he could before eventually leaving and being tried. Yemen kicked out their president for life too.

Syria's president is much more like Mubarak. Despite becoming a doctor and not even planning on becoming President for Life until his older brother died in a car accident. He had the same system of secret police and prisons that Mubarak used. Even worse (and not surprisingly) Syria was Russia's only real ally in the Middle East and hosted Russia's only Mediterranean Naval Base. When the people started agitating for change Assad started a civil war to get rid of the 'terrorists' who were trying to get rid of his illegitimate rule. This lawlessness eventually did lead to real terrorists forming their own armies to take him and the entire Western world on. When Assad used nerve gas on his own people, Obama tried to use that as a valid excuse to bomb him out of office. Unfortunately, he had to give him an out (even if nobody thought he would take it) to make it acceptable to our allies and Russia. Putin told him to give up his chemical weapons, sign the international treaty, etc. and he did. As Obama now had to follow his word and not bomb Assad and as Putin blocked any other international agreements, Syria descended into a death spiral that led to millions of refugees and the rise of Islamic State.

About a year into the Arabic Spring, I went on a trip to Jordan. Jordan is similar to Morocco in many ways. Nice, loved king whose picture is everywhere most likely out of true love by his people. He responded like the King of Morocco and is still there and still loved as well. Jordan is truly a great place to visit. Like Morocco it is neither overpopulated nor super poor. The food is amazing. It has many Biblical sites if you care for those. And the Dead Sea. The Dead Sea is so salty that you can float in it with no effort at all. Just don't get it in your eyes. And unless you have skin as tough as old saddle leather, don't believe what they tell you about how the mud from it is good for your skin. It burns. Towards the South are the ruins of the Pre-Islamic city of Petra. It is still amazing to this day. Further South is something called Wadi Rum. It is also known as the Valley of the Moon. It looks like some kind of alien landscape. It was used for filming *The Martian* & *Lawrence of Arabia*. The real Lawrence used it for a staging area as he rallied the Arabic tribes to fight the Turks in the First World War. An amazing place that takes your breath away.

In the North, we went to Jedarra. This is a small town on the Syrian border. In Jesus time it was called Gadara. He supposedly met a guy there who was possessed by many devils. He kicked them out of the guy and the ran into a herd of pigs that then drowned themselves in the river. I was hoping to have a nice ham sandwich there. I hear it is **devilishly** good ...

Unfortunately, no.

While we were enjoying our swine-free lunch we looked across the valley to Syria. If I had walked across the border, odds are I wouldn't be here to type this today.

Since the initial hope of the Arabic Spring, things have taken a turn for the worst in many of the countries. Libya is likely about to re-enter a civil war. The Shia minority in Bahrain is still out of power. Assad with Iran & Russia backing him was able to pick off all his opposition and is still settling scores. The host nations for refugees are getting less $ & media attention, so are trying to send refugees back to the smoking ruin that is much of Syria. Islamic State took over much of Iraq before being taken down. Morocco and Jordan continue slowly getting better and more democratic. Mubarak's successor was a moderate from the Islamic Brotherhood. His own incompetence and unwillingness to write a constitution that was representative of Egypt's Muslims **and** Christians gave another former Army general an excuse to become the new, younger, worse Mubarak. Yemen became even more of a Hellscape after Saudi and Iran each backed different sides to be the next government.

There is hope however. Maybe the world moved on. Maybe the democracy activists just got better and savvier. Maybe a few Presidents for Life just got too old & tired to fight back. Whatever it may be there have been 2 big successes in the Arab World. Algeria & Sudan just kicked out their Presidents for Life.

This time, they seem to be handling the transitions better in both places. Both groups of demonstrators have been able to block the government or military plans for a successor regime.

Cross your fingers, maybe the generations long Arabic Winter is nearing an end.

THE MANHATTAN CANDIDATE

If you really were a Russian agent, you could not hurt the country more than you are now.

-*The Manchurian Candidate*, book & movies

The *Manchurian Candidate* with Frank Sinatra as the lead character came out as a movie first in 1962, right before Kennedy was shot. As the movie dealt with an assassination attempt of a presidential candidate, it was pulled from the theatres for years. The second version had Denzel Washington in the lead and was updated to the first Iraq war from the original Korean War.

In the original, Sinatra gradually realizes that one of his ex-troops has been brainwashed by the Russians to kill a popular presidential candidate during the Party Convention. Then the VP candidate, who is really an idiot planted by the Russians, will take power. Before the convention the Idiot is pushed to create a (fake) controversy and get national attention by publicly stating there are communists in the State Department. This part of the plot was meant to satirize the McCarthy Red Scare Witch-hunt from the 50s.

As the Idiot continues to make his false charges, it tears the country apart just like the McCarthy hearings did.

One of his opponents tells the Idiot the quote I used as the epigraph for this story.

Our current Russian dupe and Idiot-in-Chief has been doing the same kind of shenanigans even all the way back to when Obama was president & he kept stating Obama was a Kenyan Muslim despite it being obviously a lie.

Then there is all the anti-Hispanic racism. A native-born US judge can't decide his case because he is of Hispanic origins. Rapists and murderers. MS-13. Bad hombres. Saying he will build a wall, then reneging on the promise later & saying it was just an election stunt.

And Muslims? Banned. Even banned people from Iran, which has never been involved in terrorism against us. While the oil rich Saudis who bred 17 of the 19 9-11 hijackers, not so much. Talked bad about them to no end. Kisses the ass of the bad dictators and starves the more enlightened Muslim rulers. Rarely mentions Islam without adding Fundamentalist Terrorism.

Before the election videos of Trump were the most popular ISIS recruiting tool.

Dogging various (conveniently enough) black public figures as stupid.

Saying a crowd of neo-Nazis & white supremacists has some good people in it.

Whether the Idiot-in-Chief really is being blackmailed by Putin to do what he wants is irrelevant. It has been shown they tried (and succeeded) in getting him elected. He obviously is not a candidate for brainwashing, you need one of those to wash it.

But the epigraph is still true:

If you really were a Russian agent, you could not hurt the country more than you are now.

The book & movies all have a happy ending. Sinatra/Denzel gets to the brainwashed guy & un-brainwashes him. Then he of his own free will takes out the Idiot at the convention.

Too bad Frank ain't around no more …

Denzel, want the role of a lifetime?

THE POODLE

Got the world up my ass
And I'm gonna jump fast
Be the first
Won't be the last
I've got the world up my ass
Twisted mind, withered brain
You know I'm going insane
I've got the world up my ass

-from the song *I've Got the World Up My Ass* by the
Circle Jerks

Before the late 60s, if you were crazy, you got locked up in a mental
hospital and they threw away the key. 'Crazy' back then included
things like mental retardation. There were few safeguards and
people were restrained in straitjackets for prolonged periods, heavily
medicated, given shock therapy (which can sometimes help at the
expense of memory for severe depression) or even lobotomies. My
favorite lobotomy technique is to take a *sterilized* knitting needle
(we are healers dammit, of course we sterilize it first!) and slip it
under the eyelid then straight back to the brain & jiggle it around
in there. Doesn't make you less crazy, but you tend to be a little
more mellow afterward. JFK's sister got one. All the cool people were
getting lobotomies back then … some clown won a Nobel Prize for
inventing it. Not surprisingly, there was a backlash once this became
public. Even if it can be a valid last resort for severe untreatable

depression, shock therapy will never make it back to being popular again. Restraints are heavily reviewed. Lobotomies are extinct. The book and later Jack Nicholson movie (his best IMO), *One Flew Over the Cuckoo's Nest* was the death knell of the old way of doing things.

Now to be locked up in a psychiatric hospital against your will under California legal code section 5150, you must be determined to be a danger to yourself or others or gravely disabled to the point you can't provide for your basic needs. You can only be placed on one by police, a psychiatrist or someone who is specially trained. These people are called the PET team (Psychiatric Evaluation Team). They only last 3 days. You have to go back to court to get another for more 2 weeks. Long term involuntary psychiatric hospitalizations are very hard to get. Recently, the pendulum is swinging back, and it is getting easier to involuntarily long term hospitalize people with a documented chronic mental illness, multiple hospitalizations and proven failure to make it long term on their own.

This has led to an explosion of homeless psychiatric patients on the street. In a normal economy, 90% of homeless are mentally ill, alcoholics, drug addicts or a combo thereof. This is why I never give them $. Even giving them food can just mean they have more free $ for alcohol or drugs. At worst, it goes into a bottle or a crack pipe. At best, it allows them to survive more comfortably on the streets without taking their (FREE) psych meds or going to AA and getting their life in order. They also flood into the ERs because they know if they say they are suicidal, they get 3 days of food, clothing and shelter at your tax $s' expense. Some people know how to work the system. Some have been placed on a 5150 over 50 times and never figured out how to off themselves. One ER doc I used to work with had one of these guys there for his twice weekly psych eval. He pulled the curtain & told the guy: 'OK, you've been suicidal every time I've ever seen you and you're 50. Bullshit. If you want me to believe you, the street is right outside, go play in traffic!' Unethical as hell, but then this guy is. But understandable.

In a normal ER without a separate psych ER, you get labs to see if they are medically safe to go to a psychiatric hospital and make sure it isn't all caused by drugs. Then you call the PET store. Depending on how good their insurance is and how much crazy is out there it may take days to get someone out to even decide if they need a 5150. Then maybe even up to a week to find a psych hospital that will take them. Some hospitals will even pay the bill for the psych hospital to get them out of the ER. If you are pregnant, blind, teenaged or in a wheelchair; it is almost impossible to place you. A combo is the kiss of death.

So, this guy came in with an ambulance (another $1500 or so of your taxes) because he had a poodle up his ass & knew if it came out, he would die. Of course, he is a schizophrenic. We did the labs and called the PET store only to be told you are allowed to think you have a poodle up your ass as long as you don't plan on putting a shotgun up there to get rid of it. Nice.

Since then, although I wish I'd thought of it for this guy, in similar situations I have the nurses give a little psych meds in a shot before they leave to help get rid of the poodles (or whatever the dysfunction may be). And it has the benefit of keeping them out of my ER a little longer. Win for me and the patient.

On my way home, I kept thinking of this guy. Before I left, I told his nurse, appropriately named Fanny, the plan on him. Ms. Fanny was a moderately attractive girl and was one of those nurses you can tell spends at least 30 minutes in front of the mirror at home before work. Great plan when you're working with a lot of alcoholics, psych patients, etc. that you REALLY don't want hitting on you … When the lab does a blood test there is usually a little left over and you can ask them to run an extra test on that without the need for poking the patient again. They can do blood levels of alcohol and all kinds of medicines.

I called back to the ER during my long drive home and asked for Fanny. I asked her to do me a favor. She said: 'Of course Dr. Wade, what?' I told her to call the lab and ask if they could add on a test for the patient. She asked which test & I told her a blood poodle level.

Ungrateful little girl hung up on me. The nerve.

THE POOTY BOOTY CALL

booty call: Noun. A late night summons – often made via telephone – to arrange clandestine sexual liaisons on an ad hoc basis.

-Urban Dictionary definition

We've all heard the rumors that Trump paid a Russian prostitute to pee in front of him for his sexual pleasure. Nice. Unfortunately (as I am a Trump hater), these seem to be not very credible allegations.

Pee games are a well-known 'perversion'. They even come in 2 kinds: **indoor,** in which someone is getting pee into their mouth or X ... and **outdoor,** where someone is getting peed on. Although, as pee games are not about SEX, they are about POWER, it does seem within the realm of possibility that an insecure megalomaniac who likes having his way with unwilling women would get off (literally) on making some poor prostitute do that. And his buddy Vlad could be trusted to NOT show anyone (besides Wittle Donny as part of a little blackmail), the tapes. THAT could explain why Trump always covers for Putin and Russia despite copious evidence that Putin is a monster.

Regardless of the truth about peeing whores, I envision a little scene happening in Helsinki right about now:

Alternating between Putin's and Wittle Donny's rooms at the Helsinki Hilton:

PUTIN: (picks up phone and dials Wittle Donny's room) Hey girl, what you doingk?

WITTLE DONNY: (rubbing his wittle pig eyes, in footie pyjamas) Sleepin'.

PUTIN: You comingk to my room right now.

WITTLE DONNY: Yes, SIR! (Runs from room)

Putin's Room less than a minute later:

WITTLE DONNY: What do you want, SIR? (saluting)

PUTIN: You to hold still while standingk on plastic sheets at end of bed.

WITTLE DONNY: Yes, SIR! (nearly falling over himself getting in position) Now what, SIR?

PUTIN: You holdingk very still right now. (whips IT out and pees all over Wittle Donny)

BOTH: AAHHHHHH!!!!! (in a very satisfied way)

PUTIN: You goingk back to your room now. Daddy want sleep, no cuddle.

WITTLE DONNY: Ok, SIR! (runs outta room leaving a snail trail of Pootie pee after him) …

Fade to black with sounds of contented Pootie snoring.

THE PREDATOR

There's no stoppin what can't be stopped
No killin what can't be killed...
There's somethin out there waitin for us
You can run but you can't hide
From the Westside night stalker, shit talker

-partial lyrics from *The Predator* by Ice Cube

I first saw the Predator when his wife was brought in after trying to OD on **his** psych meds. Despite the situation, he was dressed overly nice for being in the ER. And he was too slick overall. The kind that you can tell is somehow fake. I didn't even realize the reason he was in & assumed at first he might be someone from hospital administration. I noticed him being too flirty with one of the nicer looking nurses. While he was in for his wife's OD …

Later he kept coming in with one of his buddies from AA who kept smoking & using meth despite being at death's door because of it. And every time he lied about being sober at first. The friend later died in some hotel room alone as best as we could figure out. Later The Predator got outta line at another hospital ER and was kicked out by security. They restrained him and cracked a rib in the process. He kept coming back to ours for the pain from that. For fun, as he told me later, he would go 'take out' meth dealers in the desert to the East of LA.

He is an alcoholic and addict with bipolar disorder. And former military with at least a little PTSD from the sounds of it. Even worse, from what I can tell, he had **antisocial personality disorder**, also known as sociopathy. People with this tend to have addiction problems and get in trouble with the law frequently. A huge proportion of jail inmates are sociopaths. They were raised without being given unconditional love at an early age so cannot feel empathy or care about others like regular people can. An old ER saying is: 'Borderlines are the patients you want to kill; sociopaths are the ones who want to kill you.' Not people to mess with.

As he kept coming back, I noticed his pattern and at first tried to subtly push him to being taken care of by the Physician Assistant (PA) on duty at the time since he never came in with anything serious & was very needy and difficult to please. Eventually I realized this was actually making my life harder as he was too much for the PAs to handle and ended up seeing him myself when he came in. As always, I run a tight ship and don't let manipulative people manipulate me. Because I was firm but fair and still took the time to talk to him, he ended up respecting me. But he would still drop little hints or remarks that let you know he could go off if you rubbed him the wrong way. And that would have been a big problem.

The last time I saw him was shortly after his AA buddy died. His wife was back from the psych hospital but things were still kinda weird there. He had a minor broken bone so I ended up giving him an Rx for narcotic pain pills. And he didn't have an AA sponsor. He seemed to be in a pretty tough place and we ended up talking a lot. I did my best to make sure he was gonna be OK in his sobriety with the Rx. I encouraged him to get a new AA sponsor. When he told me that he had got rid of his last one because he was trying to use him as had most everyone he had cared for in his entire life, I told him that most people aren't actually bad and he had to keep at it. I gave him the Buddhist explanation for why people act badly: Very few people are intentionally evil. Most are trying to do the right thing but can't because they were raised by rabid wolves who put cigarettes out on their butt or whatever the specifics may be.

Before he left, he told me that I was the only one at the ER who treated him right & gave me his card for the private security company he runs. I am sure he is good at it. And pretty sure that he would put someone in the hospital if you paid him for it. Since I have no need for a bodyguard and wouldn't entirely trust him not to turn on me if I said the wrong thing, I didn't keep the card.

I did however keep him in my memory. It is truly flattering that this dangerous guy felt grateful to me just for treating him with a little respect.

The registration girls saw how I was extra attentive to this always sharply dressed guy & asked me if he was a movie star or something.

My reply was that he is a very dangerous person, so it is best to handle him gently …

THE (REAL) HERO

The Hero (movie 2017) Sam Elliot, Laura Prepon. An ailing movie star comes to terms with his past and mortality.

-IMDb description

I met The Hero at the end of last year. He is almost my age of 50. He was quiet and thoughtful with kind of a rugged cowboy vibe. And not the cluelessly independent, full speed ahead at what **I** want type of 'cowboy' that Americans are so infamous for being abroad. We were full, so I talked to him about what was going on in the lobby as we cleared a bed for him in the Evaluation and Treatment Center (ETC) at my job at a National Cancer Center. He had brought some kind of spy novel to read for what he knew would be the inevitable wait time. Smart. Better than those people who complain every 5 minutes like a 7-year old on a long car trip: 'Are we there yet?'. But then I'm a big reader, so I'm biased.

We have **the** most advanced cancer treatments available pretty much anywhere in the world. If we don't have at least a hopefully promising study drug and can't cure your cancer, it likely can't be cured, at least at this point in time. Not that we cure everybody mind you, but all our patients get their best chance.

As I reviewed The Hero's chart before really talking to him, I saw that he had been told we had no likely cure for him. The best we could offer would be palliative chemotherapy. It might give him a few months, but at a cost of baldness, vomiting, diarrhea and susceptibility to infections that could even kill him before the cancer would. His doctor wrote a slightly pointed or miffed note in his chart that he had steadfastly refused all chemo. He had already had some kind of chemo pump implanted in his belly by a surgeon at an outside facility early in the course of his treatment before he came to us.

He had had a fever off and on for a month. Given that it was slowly progressing with no other symptoms, it was likely that the hardware in his belly was infected & would need to be removed to really stop the fevers. Not a big deal as it was no longer being used. Or maybe it was just a fever because of his cancer. Regardless, not something we could tell in the ETC, especially at nite. It would require something pretty invasive like a camera down his throat to his gallbladder or surgery to prove that. The best we could do was basic lab tests & an X-Ray to look for anything obviously wrong and give him some antibiotics to cover the presumed source. Anything more would require being admitted for several days and lots of tests.

I told him this and asked him what he wanted to do, especially as he had drove or more likely as I found out later took his bike down from a couple hours away and would be stranded down in LA. This was even more problematic considering the incurable status of his disease and his previous wishes. He was very matter of fact about knowing his prognosis and accepting it. He took the right choice (in my humble opinion), of doing the tests, getting the antibiotics and planning on going home as long as there was no obvious other infection worth being admitted for. He planned on talking to his original surgeon back home about how long it would put him down if he had the hardware taken out. It was kinda cramping his style anyway. It was hard for him to move as freely as he'd like with this big piece of plastic in his belly.

As he still had some time to wait & was just a cool stand up kind of guy with a great attitude, I asked him if he had seen the movie *The Hero* & later brought him the Amazon Prime pages with the movie's details when he said that he hadn't. In the movie, Sam Elliot plays a minor character cowboy actor of a certain age who's already not very special life is thrown for a loop when he is told he has incurable pancreatic cancer & the best he can hope for is some additional time if he gets surgery to remove what they can. Then he meets the much younger and hotter Laura Prepon who falls for **him** and gives him a reason to live and get the surgery. I knew he could relate. He appreciated the tip. He was also a standup guy in his attitude to his wife. As I was telling him about the movie and how it tracked pretty close to where he was at, I somewhat clumsily said: 'Of course your wife isn't Laura Prepon ...' He immediately answered back: 'My wife is beautiful.' And beamed as he proudly told me how as soon as she got out of the military, she had gotten both arms tattooed in sleeves.

After he got back in the room & was waiting for results, I spent quite a bit of time talking to him as it wasn't that busy and more importantly, because he was an interesting, admirable guy worth talking too. I would have gladly let some paper(computerized)work slide and caught up later for the chance to hang out in his room.

We talked a lot about his life since the diagnosis & prognosis. He has a projected exit date of about April. And is ok with that. Since his wife has a good job, he had the luxury to quit his own. He had used that time to get serious about motorcycle racing. To the point that he had become number one in the country in his division/event. And had a COH sticker on his bike. And talked about not blowing off possible cancer and getting screening early when he was on the road & in the spotlight for his wins.

He also told me about his surgeon and how the guy told him what his options were and then said: 'Do what you want. I don't have any personal stake in doing any particular surgery. It's up to you.' This was the first time he had heard anything like this from a doctor. He had immense respect for the guy. Most of them were telling him more along the lines of: 'You have to do this. We're gonna do this. We will fight this to the bitter end.' He didn't want a bitter end. He knew he had an end but that **the bitter was only an option**.

He asked me why so many doctors are afraid to talk about death, futility and decisions like he had made. I told him some was just that so many doctors are pushed to do nothing but study their whole lives to get into med school that they don't necessarily have much life experience or ability to think outside the box. And when they do talk too many of them can't speak except in Latin/Greek medical terms instead of English. Even native English speakers. And of course, oncologists dedicate themselves to fighting cancer. And if you spend half your life in a lab trying to cure cancer, you are the right guy for that job, but an extended conversation with something besides a test tube, not necessarily so much. And of course, many people in our culture in or out of medicine are afraid to talk about death & dying.

I fully supported him in this mature and evolved outlook and decision. We talked a lot about that. I told him about a couple of authors and some of their books and later gave him Amazon pages of them. The first was a Russian author, Alexander Solzhenitsyn. Young aspiring writers, as Sasha (Russian nickname for Alexander) S. was, are told to write what you know. So, he did. But what he knew was atrocious. He was taken as a POW by the Germans in WW2 then sent straight to Siberia after the war for writing a personal letter to a friend expressing mild doubts about Stalin's war management. While there he had a spiritual awakening and started writing. After the camps, he got cancer while still an internal exile in Siberia. He ended up winning the Nobel prize in literature in the '70s then got exiled to the West until after the fall of the USSR. His most famous book is *One Day in the Life of Ivan Denisovich*. It describes a winter day in the work camp in Siberia. The last few lines are some of the most crushingly sad but simultaneously most hopeful & inspiring I have ever read (And I've read a few books): 'It was a good day. He got some sausage from a friend's care package. He got enough tobacco to make a cigarette. He (used all his skill and did an impeccable job as he) built a wall (in the middle of Siberia that was for Stalin ultimately and might never even be used). He didn't get beaten or otherwise punished by guards … He had 3653 days like it left in his sentence. The 3 extra days are for leap years.' Damn. In his later book *The Gulag Archipelago*, Sasha gets into the mental process he went through to essentially have a Buddha-like awakening (Buddha literally means the awakened one). He lost all sense of anger at the unfair system that doomed him to the camps. He learned who he really was & what he really needed to be happy. He got a new source of self-worth from 'lowering' himself to do manual labor with the bricklayers instead of trying for a soft prison desk job with the other intellectuals. He actually was glad that he was sent to the camps because it allowed him to wake up & wouldn't give up the experience if he had the chance. He also talked about how people in the camps could go one of three ways: evolve, give up and die or become a worm/stool pigeon/trusty and give up their humanity. Only the first or last groups would likely live through the camp. But the last would not come out truly alive. He liked that & it resonated very closely with where he was at and the decisions he had made. We talked about how you **can** have a good day even in a Siberian work camp. And it is entirely dependent on your attitude. If a good day is to be had in a Siberian work camp, a good day can be had anywhere. **It is up to you.**

Next, I told him about Viktor Frankl. Vik was an Austrian Jewish psychoanalyst a generation younger than Freud. He could have escaped before WW2 but wanted to stay for his family so got sent to Dachau. His book is *Man's Search for Meaning*. In it he comes to strikingly similar conclusions and has a similar awakening. In different language he pins the ability to survive on finding something meaningful to you to carry you through. Kinda like Sasha's building a wall. And he saw the same division into the awakened, the hopeless and the worms among his fellow prisoners. We talked about how an experience like that can offer you a chance to show what you are really made of. And how in many senses COH is a concentration/work camp where the odds are against you, but regardless of whether or not you leave on both feet, it can be a crucible for your soul that refines you to your true essence.

I see the same 3 response mechanisms every day at work. There are the patients (and family members) who take it like a man (or woman). Those passive ones who don't even necessarily go to all their appointments, much less fight a good fight. And there are the ones who use cancer as a way to get high on pain meds for free or just become even more difficult and unpleasant than they were before the diagnosis. It's hard to judge, you rarely know what turned the last 2 groups into the kind of people they are or their capacity to change for the better under trying circumstances. It is easy to respect those who go out with their boots still on though.

I also told him about the book *The Plague* by the French Nobel winner Alfred Camus. It tells a fictionalized version of one of the last modern massive outbreaks of the Bubonic Plague/Black Death in a small North African town where Camus grew up as a colonial. After the city is quarantined the bodies start piling up and a small band of accidental friends become instrumental in dealing with the situation. Of course, there are mass graves, dead rats and buboes aplenty, but Camus was an Existentialist. This means that he believed that in a world where God may not even exist, it is up to each individual to decide what he thinks is the best, most honorable way to live. And his characters again get broken into the same 3 types. All the more interesting when you consider that Camus never went to a camp like Sasha & Vik did.

I also told him about the first 2 rules of the Buddha which can be seen in different language in all the big world religions. #1: All life involves suffering. True. And #2: All suffering is caused by an unhealthy attachment to having things go your way. Little harder to carry that one out, but the effort to let go is worthy in and of itself. Not everyone can be a Buddha. But my buddy The Hero is.

As he told me about how he was going to a meditation teacher to become a better person, I printed him out a few stories I had written about Buddhism and meditation among other things. [*Holidays in Cambodia & Indian Food for the Body (and Soul?)*] Again, it was appreciated and what he needed. If I do say so myself.

His tests came back without any obvious badness, so he got some IV antibiotics and a script for more and headed home with a little validation and food for thought. When I went up to the nurses' station to tell his nurse (new to COH) the plan, she told me how he really liked me and was impressed because most doctors don't spend time really talking to their patients. I told her about how he had an exit date in April and wanted to go out with the most quality of life, rather than do futile chemo for a few miserable extra months. She whimpered and almost cried. A more seasoned (jaded/numbed?) COH nurse told her, it's OK, you're new here …

THERE'S A BONE THERE?!?

Sticks & stones shall break my bones, but words will never hurt me.

-nursery Rhyme

One day I had a 50ish non-English speaking Chinese guy come in because of a 'penis problem'. It turns out he was having sex with his wife and one zigged while the other zagged and he ended up with a broken penis.

And no, there is not a bone there, unless you are a whale. And no, that does not count that fat butt-white guy at the beach. There are actually 3 tubes full of spongy blood vessels in the penis. You get excited and the exit for the blood gets shut off & Mr. Happy gets bigger as the tubes swell. Rarely, fortunately, if you are moving out of synch or un-lubricated, (You would think Harvey Weinstein, et al would have this happen every other week. Would serve them right.) you can break the sheath of one of the tubes and the penis gets swollen, purple and bent. The medical descriptive term for this is an Eggplant Deformity. Look it up on Google images now & get back to me. Not a pretty image or actuality, right? Bad juju. It can be repaired with surgery, but that's not on anyone's bucket list. I hope. But then as a comedian once said: 'There are something like 7 Billion people on this planet. Try to wrap your head around that. Among other things, this means ANYTHING you can imagine & shit you can't even imagine is being done by more than 1 person on this planet right now. There are probably several people right now with jumper cables and a car battery hooked up to their junk right now & LIKING it!'

This poor guy got taken to surgery right away by the urologist and I hope he did OK. My attention was drawn however to the guy's son. He was maybe about 25. Since he could speak English fluently & we had no translator available then, he had to translate the story for us. And see his dad's eggplant. And imagine his mom & dad getting freaky …

Try to imagine how disturbing that would be to you. I hope he isn't still in therapy.

UGLY BETTY

Never judge a book by its cover.

-old saying

'Betty Luna' was a frequent flier at all of our local ERs for years. Everyone was on a first name basis with her. To look at her, Betty was pretty revolting. Over 300 pounds, butt white, greasy white hair pulled back in a little pony tail. Her only clothes were a set of matching grey sweatshirt & sweatpants. She was schizophrenic which meant she smoked like crazy (appropriately enough). Over 90% of schizophrenics do. Someone found a mechanism by which schizophrenics specifically are calmed by nicotine more than your average smoker. Not to mention the poor impulse control and judgment that goes with being schizophrenic. And it is actually encouraged in psychiatric hospitals because the staff knows it makes their job easier.

Between the obesity and the smoking, she had emphysema and heart failure and her blood pressure was always dangerously high. Of course, she never took her psych meds, much less those for her blood pressure, etc. Worse, because she was obese, the smoking, the heart failure and just plain not taking care of herself she had chronically swollen lower legs and feet. Both shins had chronic deep ulcers that always had at least some infection and were oozing pus or at least fluid from the open skin.

Because of her mental illness Betty could get very touchy and nasty if you pushed her or if it was just a Bad Betty Day. Once she was in the cafeteria and apparently thought it would be funny to pour hot water or coffee down the back of the neck of some other person using the cafeteria. This led to her being banned from coming into the hospital outside of the ER for months. Hospitals are forbidden to refuse anyone at least stabilizing care who shows up at the ER. Occasionally, with a long well documented record of the police being called for a patient's behavior multiple times, it is possible to ban someone from an ER, but that is very rare. And her **sleep in a patient bed or in a chair in the lobby after being seen privileges** were revoked.

This of course was a big problem because as far as anybody could tell, she was homeless and slept in an ER every night if she could. She was cagey enough to know that if she said that she was homeless, then that would mean social workers would start trying to place her in some facility. And her schizophrenic paranoia sure didn't want **that**. She would nearly always refuse any tests or care, much less admission to the hospital which was always needed for her various problems. And of course, she wasn't going to let us give her any psych meds. To truly get rid of the ulcers on her legs she would need to be admitted for weeks or months to a long term rehab hospital for IV antibiotics, special dressings and wound care, possible surgery, and of course to get her other problems treated enough to let the legs heal. There is a very good public rehab hospital in LA County that would have been perfect for her. That wasn't gonna happen. A few times she agreed to let me do tests. Usually she reneged on the deal after agreeing. Once she even got nasty with the (too sweet for her own good) nurse who was trying to do an EKG on her. She threw the EKG cables at her and stormed out. I think I was able to talk her into staying in the hospital once. And we heard rumors after her periodic disappearances for a few weeks at a time that they were caused by her being admitted to some other hospital. Once, even at the next County Hospital from LA County, over an hour away. As I said Betty was surprisingly cagey and able to get around well despite her issues. She knew all the ins and outs of getting by on the fringes of society. She told me once about how one particular church had an open store for the homeless where they gave whatever they had for free to people like her between such and such hours one day a week. She knew how to keep herself in the basics.

The only thing she ever really wanted from us was dressing material and bandages for her weeping legs. They needed to be changed several times a day. Sometimes she would try to get a Tylenol #3 for her leg pain, but I would tell her she needed to let us do tests and stay for something like that to happen. Since the reaction against the massive abuses of psychiatric patients that lasted up until the late 60s, it has been very difficult to force psych patients to stay in a psych hospital. They need to meet strict criteria of danger to self, danger to others or be gravely disabled to the point that they cannot provide for their basic food, clothing & shelter. While Betty was truly a danger to herself, it was of the slow kind that would not meet criteria for a psychiatric hold.

As I mentioned and have detailed at length Betty was repulsive in her behavior and appearance. But there was a softer side of Betty. She could be very sweet when it was a Good Betty Day. Once she got to know you, she would tell her favorite staff members 'I love you'. One of the nurse supervisors, who smoked as well, spent extra time with Betty as they were often both outside smoking regularly. She told me that Betty once asked her if she wanted to go out together. Betty volunteered to teach her how to rob graves. Dunno if this was intended to be a date or just friends hanging out and I hope Betty wasn't really robbing graves, but you never know. And the hospital staff and probably a few people in the church store, etc. were the closest thing Betty had to friends or real relationships

She was essentially retarded, for want of a more politically correct word. Eventually all schizophrenics develop something more or less like dementia. It is part of the disease and the brain physically atrophies and shrinks due to the lack of much real thought or life content during their entire adult life. The earlier you get schizophrenia, the worse it is. John Nash, the real guy from the movie *A Beautiful Mind,* didn't come down with it until college or grad school. He went on to get a Ph. D. in math & win a Nobel Prize. And his life was still shattered.

Betty told one of the nurses once that she started hearing voices when she was 7. For all intents and purposes, her mental development stopped there. She was child-like and able to navigate the system well after doing it for all of her 50 some years, but she was quite limited. Heartbreakingly tragic if you think about it.

As I like to keep my ER as drama free as possible, I developed a routine with Betty. As soon as I heard she was in the lobby, I would get her a sandwich, juice and a blanket and bring it to her. Then I would say hi and ask if she wanted to be seen or just get the dressing material, which she always put on herself. Nearly all the time she just took the dressing stuff. Gradually I became one of her 'I love you' recipients. Once she even gave me some childish Disney Valentine's Day stickers she had gotten from someone. They were of various Disney characters in hearts, etc. with 'I love you!' on them. Not my style, but I couldn't refuse them. About that time, I started replying to her 'I love you's with 'I love you too Betty'. I brought them home and gave them to my wife after telling her about Betty. Pretty sure we still have one on our address book at home.

On a Bad Betty Day it was almost impossible to talk to her. She would get very irritable and go onto rants about whatever was bothering her or someone (maybe imaginary) who wasn't treating her well. I was able to talk her down a little sometimes on those days by asking her what was happening and telling her 'I love you', but those days she usually ended up just leaving early while grumbling on her way out the door.

The beginning of the end came one day when I heard that the last time Betty was in the ER, she had maggots coming out of the ulcer on one leg. Maggots are fortunately pretty rare in the ER. Usually it is someone with chronic leg wounds like Betty. And, of course, homeless with a side of alcoholism or mental illness that would let you ignore your health long enough and bad enough that flies lay eggs there that are allowed to turn into maggots. Maggots only eat dead flesh so they are actually not that bad for you, but the conditions that let them get there are obviously horrible for you. A cutting edge wound treatment is to use **sterile** maggots to clean out only the dead tissue. At that I knew and told people that she would be dead within a year.

Betty kept coming in for a while and fortunately remained maggot free. But her blood pressure and breathing kept getting worse. Regardless, she refused tests, treatment and admission. Her blood pressure was in the low 200s all of the last times I saw her. Then she stopped coming for months at a time. When she did make her increasingly rare appearances, she looked haggard and bad.

Most of the last 6 months or so, we only heard rumors about her. That she was in the ICU at USC County Hospital, etc. The last verified Betty sighting was from a friend at his other ER job. She supposedly had a heart rate of 200 and was allowed/encouraged to sign out Against Medical Advice. In my book, this was malpractice, as in that case she could have easily been dead within hours. But it wasn't my decision and I can sympathize. Betty was an unappealing handful to deal with. It has been a year or maybe even 2 since more than a flimsy rumor of a Betty sighting. I am pretty sure she is taking the dirt nap now. At least she is at peace. She rarely had anything like peace in her troubled life.

I LOVE YOU BETTY!!!

UNCONVENTIONAL MEDICINE

Normal healthy people feel sick when they see violence. We are trying to help you become healthy. Consider this a side effect of your treatment.

-Clockwork Orange, the book and movie

During the 2016 Repugnantican Presidential Convention, there was an outbreak of the viral stomach flu among several attendees.

Pity.

This virus tends to flare up in late summer, especially in places like cruise ships where there are large groups of people in small quarters to spread the highly contagious virus. It causes vomiting and diarrhea and is not very fun. The only resemblance to the normal coughing, etc. flu, is in the name & the fact that they are both caused by viruses. It did not hit the Democratic Convention.

I do not think this was a coincidence.

The Great Orange Beast 666 was their candidate. You may say I am being a little dramatic calling him the Biblical Beast/Anti-Christ from the Book of Revelations. I however can base my contention on solid Biblical evidence. And that book was divinely inspired and 100% true, right?

Revelations 13:18 Thou shalt know the Number of the Beast for it is a human number. It is 666.

Revelations 13:16 The Beast and his followers shall wear the Number of the Beast, either on their hands or on their foreheads (which they must attempt to cover with the world's worst combover-eth).

Come on, could any human with eyes (including the Shithole in Chief), really think that thing looks good? And he is a stable genius (just ask him) so there must be a good reason for it. (There is an alternate version of **Rev. 13:18**. Thou shalt know the Color of the Beast for it is NOT a human color. It is: ORANGE.) The Book of Revelations also mentions the False Prophet who shall come before the Beast and prepare the way for him. Anyone ever hear of this thing called Fox News? Also, one of the classic names for the Devil is the Lord of Lies. In Christian theology Jesus is not only the Son of God, he is considered indistinguishable from God himself. The same must apply to the relationship between the Devil and the Anti-Christ. Try fact checking nearly anything he says ...

I think I have made my case. Back to the convention. As could be implied by the epigraph I chose, I think the fact that a bunch of Repugnanticans puking and shitting themselves at the party to celebrate the candidacy of Shithole is a good thing. Normal people feel like vomiting when they see or hear that Thing. The virus was doing them a favor. It was helping them become healthier. As food that is poisoned or rotten can be fatal, evolution has made the association between vomiting and aversion to what caused it a very strong memory. Anyone feel like volunteering to lick envelopes at the Repugnantican Party headquarters next time they get stomach flu?

As to how and why it became a problem at the Repugnantican and not the Democratic Party Convention, I have a theory as well. Shithole is a notorious racist. Especially against Latinos. His party is less so, but while they and he don't want **those** people here, they are more than happy to underpay them for taking care of their golf courses, gardens, cooking, cleaning, etc.

Who do you think was running the kitchens and serving the food at the convention? Pretty sure they looked more like Cesar Chavez than your average butt white Repug. If I was in that kitchen, I know for a fact that everything that left it would have a little extra somethin' somethin'.

Revenge is a dish best served with a little essence of Manuel's ball sack as I've always said ...

WHAT A SWEET LADY

Borderlines are the ones you want to kill. Antisocials are the ones who want to kill you.

-Common expression in medicine

Borderline Personality Disorder is a serious problem. As it is a **Personality Disorder**, this means it is not like depression or anxiety that can come and go throughout your life. It is part of what you ARE. Borderline & Antisocial Personality both come from bad parenting where you grow up without a basic sense of love, caring & self-worth due to not getting exposed to them as a very young child. Men tend to be the fighting, stealing, violent, criminal Antisocials. Women tend to be the seductive, unpredictable, manipulative Borderlines. Maybe this is just because of the overall socialization and expectations put on children at a young age. Little girls are still taught to catch a man & raise a family. Little boys are encouraged to fight & be tough.

Regardless, borderlines can be very tiring. They are always trying to find something to fill the big emotional void inside themselves, so will get into all kinds of things to feel (temporarily) good. Sex, drugs, alcohol, gambling, food, spending. The sex one led to the saying: 'Sex with a borderline is the best sex you will ever have, but you will pay for it for years.' They tend to do something called splitting where they will set people against each other & of course they get to be the go between to the 2 now warring camps. They also tend to over idealize or denigrate others. You can go from being the White Knight and Jesus himself to the Devil from the Fiery Pit in about 3 and ½ seconds. The 'crazy' women in the movies *Fatal Attraction* & *Basic Instinct* are both almost textbook accurate depictions of borderlines.

But anyway, one day in residency I saw this sweet lady who was there for a shoulder sprain after 'her brother with psych issues hurt it.' She was a few years older than me and reasonably attractive. And as they said in *Pulp Fiction*: 'personality goes a long way.' I was completely charmed by this sweet victim.

I ordered some pain meds and an X-ray then moved on to the next task. Then one of the nurses told me the police wanted to talk to me about the sweet lady. This is pretty common in assaults. They need to build a criminal case & interview witnesses, etc. Knowing this often leads to being subpoenaed to testify, I always tell the cops my name is spelled: D-O-N-O-T-S-U-B-P-O-E-N-A.

When I went to talk to them, they told me that the brother is not the one with psych issues, the sweetie IS. She is bipolar & her brother twisted her arm to get the knife she was trying to stab him with away from her. I took a few minutes to process this and then went to see Sweetie Pie.

As soon as I started asking her about the police's side of things, it was like the end of a Scooby Doo episode where they catch the bad guy and he pulls off the monster mask he was wearing the whole time. Except she tore off the Sweetie Pie mask she was wearing. Underneath was this frightening, screaming monster from the deepest pit of Hell. She got tied down, sedated and ended up in the psych ward for at least a few days.

That was my first encounter with a borderline. Unfortunately, not the last. But now I know what to look for and can recognize them from miles away.

WITH THIS RING I THEE SOMETHING

A **cock ring** or **cockring** is a ring worn around the penis, usually at the base. The primary purpose of wearing a cock ring is to restrict the flow of blood from the erect penis in order to produce a stronger erection or to maintain an erection for a longer period of time.

-Wikipedia definition

Guys always want to have a bigger longer lasting erection. This is why Viagra, etc. are popular even among guys who don't have impotence. These guys are in for a REALLY nasty surprise if they aren't lucky. If you take Viagra when you don't need it, you are at risk for something called priapism. A permanent erection. Sounds good, until you think it through. An erection starts when spongy parts of the penis have the blood out valve turned off because you are getting excited. If the blood can never get out, eventually the penis will start to have insufficient blood flow. After too long, it can never get hard again. The treatment involves a big needle shoved into each side of it first for numbing medicine (which doesn't work until after the needle is in of course) then to drain out the stagnant blood and inject stuff to shrink it. Doesn't that just sound fun now? In theory, an ER doctor can do this, but I don't plan on ever doing it. The urologist can get his butt outta bed and come in for that ...

Another option to keep the blood in longer is to put a cockring on the base of your penis. This lets you get a little harder for longer. But just like unnecessary Viagra, it can cut off blood flow out of the penis and cause all kinds of problems. The 'smart' cockring users use ones made of rubber. This way when the penis gets bigger and you are done, it is easy to get off. The 'dumb' ones will use some kind of steel. Macho men only use steel cockrings, ya know. Or even better something near unbreakable like titanium. Of course, when the penis gets bigger, the cockring that fit at normal size can often not be removed.

This poor guy came in because he had broken up with his wife recently. He decided to go for broke and visit a prostitute. The pro suggested a cockring. The guy figured, hey he's already going to a pro, why not? So, he did. And he did her. Then he attempted to take off the cockring. He didn't because he couldn't.

So he kept trying. He got it off a few DAYS later. Then came straight to the ER.

By then it was too late. His penis had a bend near the base that wasn't supposed to be there. There was a track oozing pus all the way around the penis where the ring used to be. He got antibiotics and we called the urologist. Regardless, I am pretty sure Mr. Happy hasn't been happy since then …

But before I leave Penisland, let me tell you about one more and it's follow up. A friend of mine in school had a patient with a very special piercing that had gone bad. It was called a Prince Albert. These involve a bar or ring that pierces straight through the shaft of the penis from one side to the other. This guy's patient had one that had gotten infected. Of course, the piercing needs to be removed to get the pus out. My buddy took it out. As soon as it was out, a nice fountain of pus followed it. Nice.

The other day I was at Target. I did the usual back & forth with the clerk at checkout.

Me: 'How you doing?'
Him: 'Good.'

Me: 'So good they have to pay you to be here, right?'
Him: 'It's still not too bad.'
Me (after realizing the thing on the big chain around his neck is a cockring): 'And they let you wear a cockring around your neck.'

We talked a little more & he told me that that is actually a Prince Albert. Apparently, the ring style of a Prince Albert can come shaped like a cockring to be even cooler(?). And it sounded like he had a Prince Albert above & below the waist.

Before we left, I told him about my friend and the pus fountain. You should have seen him bend over in pain imagining that ...

YOU SOLEMNLY SWEAR

I swear that the evidence that I shall give, shall be the truth, the whole truth and nothing but the truth, so help me God.

-Oath sworn by witnesses in a trial before giving testimony

My ex-wife had a screwy blood vessel in her brain. One day it bled and she had a seizure. From there she had seizures semi-regularly until the day she died. We at first had a special radiation treatment done that ideally would have killed the bad blood vessels and fixed everything. It didn't. And none of the seizure medicines worked that well. But they all had side effects, which meant she cycled through at least 5 different ones trying to find the one that worked with tolerable side effects. At the end of the whole thing I had enough experience with the new seizure meds to write a paper on them & even got it published in a big ER Medicine journal.

After several years we decided to have surgery to take out the bad blood vessel and any surrounding scarred brain to hopefully cure the seizures. As you can imagine it is not exactly simple cutting out part of someone's brain. You have to very precisely find the bad part then make sure it is something that can be lived without before you take it out. Sometimes if it is in a very delicate area, they will cut your skull open while you are awake and touch all the surrounding areas with an electrode before cutting anything so that they can make sure you can still talk etc. without that part.

194

Her version of this was simpler as it was a less important area. They had to put an IV in her neck and give her some kind of sedative then see if she could still talk etc. with the bad side of her brain asleep. As long as that worked, she was safe for the surgery.

Our insurance sucked then. And all insurance (or really any big) companies suck in general. They are cheap bastards who will do anything they can to block payment on things and make it hard to actually talk to a person to complain.

The pre-surgical test that she needed is called neuropsychiatric testing for billing purposes. This is pretty vague and could potentially mean just talking to a therapist about your feelings re: surgery. But it is thousands of dollars since it is a very involved procedure.

We were getting to the end of everything and then the insurance denied payment on the neuropsychiatric testing. They kept denying it. Finally, I got the surgeon's secretary to give me the name and phone number of the insurance company denial goon. I called her up after hours and left a message. And since her message was so kind as to leave the extension for her supervisor in case, she wasn't available, I left one with him too.

My message was this: 'Hi. This is Dr. Jeff Wade, husband of XXXXX Wade. Apparently, you have made a mistake. The neuropsychiatric testing you have denied is not talking to some shrink. It is to see if she can still talk after they cut part of her brain out. You WILL be approving this NOW. Or I will be talking to your boss and your boss's boss next. And if she has another seizure and falls in front of a bus & dies or otherwise hurts herself, which can happen with every seizure she has, before we can get the surgery thanks to your delay; YOU will be solemnly swearing in a court of law. Thank You, Have a nice day.'

By the time I got up and called the surgeon the next morning, it was approved.

HE'S NUMBER ONE!

Common Sense isn't (Common, that is).

-old saying

The guy who graduated first in my med school class was an OK guy. At least he wasn't one of those people who sat in the front row of every class and asked multiple stupid questions that made everyone want to kill them for wasting their time &/or making their ears bleed. He went to most of the parties and got a few girls. But then there was the fact that he was rumored to read every set of lecture notes 7 times before the test. And as they say, you are known by the company you keep.

His best buddy was someone I will call number 2. And not because he graduated 2nd in the rankings. More because it is convenient. And he was a nasty sh***y little human being. And one other reason I will get to later. You didn't see him at many parties. And I'm almost positive he didn't get any girls.

At my school, you are allowed to take exams in the lab room where you had your desk relying on the honor system to prevent cheating. And for the second year, you can request your friend to be your neighbor. These 2 picked each other. Their lab desks were connected at one end to each other.

One exam day we saw these two (both of whom were pocket sized little guys) mutually carrying in a cardboard partition that they must have cut out of a refrigerator box and was nearly as big as either of them. It had been perfectly cut to fit in the slot between their adjoining desks. Imagine how much of their so-so precious study time that must have wasted.

We asked them what that was for & their answer was that they were going to use it to prevent them looking at each other during the test and freaking each other out. Really? Nice. Wow.

Halfway through the 3rd year of school, we got the news that #2 had colon cancer that had already spread. He was going to and did end up dying shortly thereafter. It turned out he had Ulcerative Colitis (UC) that had caused his colon cancer. I for one didn't miss him.

UC and Crohn's Disease are 2 diseases where your immune system attacks your intestines causing pain, diarrhea, bloody stool, etc. UC as the name implies is limited to the colon. Crohn's can be anywhere from the lips to the ass. Not fun stuff. Together they are called Inflammatory Bowel Disease (IBD). UC has the extra fun side effect of turning into colon cancer early and people with it are recommended to have their colon surgically removed before they have had it for 10 years to prevent cancer.

Both are associated with controlling, OCD type personalities. In my experience this seems to be very highly linked to the disease. Most of the people I have seen with it have this obsessive, micromanaging anal personality. Being anal is associated with colon disease in other words. A nice little cosmic joke, no?

Another guy in my class ended up being diagnosed with Crohn's in the first year of school and dropping out to deal with his health issues. This guy was also a rather OC kind of guy and not very pleasant to be around. I didn't miss him either. He was Jewish and there is a tendency to push hard for academic success in Jewish families. That old stereotype of nagging Jewish mothers had to come from somewhere. He was even pretty orthodox, wearing the kippa (skullcap), requiring his wife (one year above us in school) to cover her hair in public, strictly kosher. Pretty obsessive, controlled lifestyle, no?

Number 2 was of Indian origins. Who knows how much of his short slight stature had to do with his genes & how much was from his chronic disease? But then Indian families also tend to place a rather high academic standard on their children as well. In short his being an anal little guy killed him before he could even graduate with his medical degree and enjoy (Although I tend to think most people like him never really learn how to enjoy much of anything.) the fruits of all his labor. He may have even died a virgin. Ironic. And tragic. But like I said, there was at least one person in our class who didn't shed a tear for him.

We had another untimely death before graduation. A friend just reminded me of him after me not thinking about him for 25 or so years. I'll call this guy The Prince, because that is the literal translation of his name and because that is a perfect description of him. The Prince was truly a good, nice, fun loving guy. I only got to spend one day with him by ourselves before he had his problem. I wish I had gotten to spend more time with him and had gotten to know him better. He had been seeing a chiropractor for over a year for severe headaches. When the chiropractor gave up, he went to a real MD. They found a tumor at the top of his spinal cord. I don't think it was cancerous, but it was in a shitty place. They did surgery to get it out, but he ended up on a ventilator. He never got off the vent and died shortly thereafter. That has forever biased me against chiropractors. That and the fact that there has never really been any good scientific study showing benefits from chiropractic manipulation versus placebo.

He never seemed to stress about exams, but to my knowledge, never had any problem with them. He definitely went to all the parties, if there wasn't a party, he would probably organize one. I didn't know him well enough to know about him getting any girls during school, but he definitely didn't die a virgin. He had an accident when he was younger and had lost one of his ring fingers. He loved to surprise people with his fingerless hand as a little joke. He sure wasn't mourning the loss of that finger. It was just what life handed him & he accepted it like a man. Even though he didn't have a huge circle of close friends, he was universally loved. When he died, I **did** go to his memorial party. And of course, it was a party, not just a ceremony. Everyone mourned him and missed him. And not just because it was a tragic loss or out of a sense of duty. Because he was really worth missing.

If you contrast the way #2 and The Prince lived their lives there is a huge difference. Number 2 seemed to hate the life he lived and lived only for the life he was going to have in his dreams. I have a feeling that if it had come, he wouldn't have been able to find much joy in his future life either. The Prince loved the life he lived. He enjoyed every moment of what he did have.

Both losses of young people in their school days before they could really get to start their mature lives, families and careers were tragic, of course. To me #2 was much more tragic, because he never really got to **live** in the first place. Whether I liked him or not, his case is more sad in some ways. And ironically, if he had been less OC and hence more likeable, he may never have gotten the UC which killed him. One of Nietzsche's maxims is: Love the Life You Live. He sure didn't.

When I think of The Prince I smile, even after all these years. If he had to die young, he got to live before he died. Not everybody can say that. Definitely not poor little #2. And The Prince was a much more pleasant person to be around in his brief time here. The two things are related.

Everyone who lives dies. Not everyone who dies has lived.

After #1 graduated, he went to San Diego for an Internal medicine residency. After the first year of residency (internship) all the soon to be former interns have to take the last step of the national medical licensing exam. As this was the dark ages before the internet and there were no such things as computer testing centers on every other block, everyone took the test at regional testing centers. Those of us who stayed in the LA area all went on the big day to some place in Pomona.

Aside from everyone bitching about the test, there was one other big topic that everyone was talking about. It involved #1. And it was so scandalous it made it all the way up to LA. He had to do a spinal tap on this guy who was drunk, crazy, confused, an uncooperative jerk or some such problem. Since you stick a long needle between 2 back bones and around the spinal cord to suck out some fluid to send to the lab, holding still is needed to get it done & not cause other problems.

This guy came up with a **really** bright idea. He was #1 in our class after all … he decided to give some medicine to paralyze the guy so he could get the tap done.

These medicines are related to curare, the plant extract that Amazon indigenous people use with blow darts to paralyze monkeys to catch them for dinner. They paralyze all the muscles in the body for varying times depending on the specific med used. They are mostly used to paralyze someone so you can put a breathing tube in their mouth down to the lungs and sometimes after to prevent them struggling against the ventilator. They also paralyze the muscles used to breathe, so there aren't really any other uses for it. Last I checked, breathing is fundamental. Even more than reading. And I'm a big fan of reading.

Number 1 didn't bother to do the mental math. Halfway through the tap, he realized the patient wasn't breathing and had to intubate him emergently without having any of the equipment, monitors or staff ready before he gave the paralytic. Nice.

Just goes to show you that common sense isn't really that common. And you don't pick it up studying all the time. In fact, that's probably a detriment to common sense.

You can't teach stupid. And there is more than one kind of stupid. As my buddy Forrest Gump says: 'Stupid is as Stupid does, my momma says …'

HIGH CHI

Tai Chi. Noun. A Chinese system of physical and spiritual exercises somewhat like yoga and possibly derived from or an influence on yoga.

-my definition

China is a very different place from the West. Its culture, languages, influences and worldview are nearly entirely separate from ours. The closest influence is from India due to the spread of Buddhism. They also were linked to the West by a long chain of intermediaries through the Silk Road that brought trade goods such as silk from China to the West & vice versa. Their culture and language have been the dominant influence on their neighbors. Educated Koreans study Chinese in school just like we used to study Latin. Their 'alphabet' is the main source of the Japanese one. All the languages in the area are related to Chinese in different degrees.

This may explain why the Chinese name for China, often translated as the Middle Kingdom, is more accurately translated as **the Central Kingdom (of the World)**. They tend to feel pretty superior about their culture. They did invent gunpowder, toilet paper, the printing press, the first civil service exams and maybe even the number 0 (try doing math without it) so they aren't entirely wrong. A common Chinese saying is: 'We can always fool a foreigner'. Are you listening Donald Trump? Your buddy the Chinese president thinks that about YOU. And in your case, he is right. But then my cat could fool Trump. Back on topic, they aren't alone in this however. All the big countries in the area feel that way about themselves. Koreans (who are SOO tall, right?) call Vietnamese peanuts because they are relatively short. And look at how the Japanese acted in WW2.

In a very real way, China has had a central role in my life. I learned as a kid that I was a monkey in the Chinese calendar. Monkeys are cute and very similar to us, so I took that to heart. Especially as the curious, playful, smart description they use to describe Monkey people fits well with my personality. I have more monkey figures from various places than most people. And love the Indian story *Ramayana* because of the heroic role played by the monkey god-king Hanuman. Then there is the Chinese story *Journey to the West*. *JW* is about a real historical Chinese Buddhist monk from about 650 AD who traveled alone from China to India and back to bring Buddhist scriptures to China then translated them to Chinese. Pretty impressive. In the fictional *JW* from about 1350, he has 4 fallen god/demon protectors/ students for the trip. The foremost, of course is the monkey god, Sun Wu Kwong (or just plain Monkey). He is super-powerful but always gets himself in trouble by trying to be too cute or sneaky. The book is among other things a literal example of the Buddhist phrase 'subdue the Monkey of the Mind and master the Horse of the Will' (one of the other helpers is a dragon who turns himself into a horse for the monk to ride). At the end of the book after getting multiple beat-downs for acting up, Monkey achieves Buddhahood and becomes enlightened. As someone whose big mouth or ideas get him into trouble semi-regularly, I can relate.

In medical school my girlfriend was a very smart Chinese nurse. She taught me the basics of Mandarin. In the year & a half we were together I got to see Chinese life from the inside. Unfortunately, she was too stuck in her own culture despite living here for 12 years and getting her degree, etc. here. She had trouble reading a children's book in English even though she spoke 12 dialects of Chinese thanks to her family being forced to move around so much during the Cultural Revolution. We ate some kind of Asian food at least 5 nites a week & she lived in a Chinese immigrant bubble in LA. Apparently it is against Chinese culture to put a picture of family members up in your house, only Chairman Mao is allowed. My sister had given me a portrait of herself that was made by 2 artist friends of hers and was in a museum on exhibit when we met. The exhibit was over & my sister gave me back the picture one Christmas. When I got back home, I hung it on the wall. That set off a huge fight. Finally, I gave in and put it in a closet. This (and my not being ready to settle down forever at 27 ...) drove us apart and eventually led to me breaking it off. As soon as I called it off, the portrait of my sister went back up on the wall. My old friends still refer to the Chinese nurse as Chairman Mao ...

The last 16 years I have worked in ERs in the new Chinatown of LA, the San Gabriel Valley, in Chinese owned hospitals. This has given me the chance (which I took firmly in hand) to become pretty good at Mandarin and less so at Cantonese. And to get an even deeper understanding and appreciation for Chinese culture. One of my favorite things at work is to see Chinese patients who don't speak much or any English, I ask 'Do you speak English?' when they say no or a little, I shift to their dialect of Chinese and their eyes almost pop out of their skull. I get mad props. But I put in hundreds of hours of practice and have several books of Chinese that I have read multiple times, so I deserve it ...

I have been to China twice so far. The first time was 2005. We went on a package tour with a (now bankrupt) company that offered travel for doctors and their families with a hospital visit in each of the big cities so it qualified as a business trip. We stayed in the North & Center of the country and saw all the standard tourist-y sites.

First, we went to Beijing and the Great Wall. While in Beijing we noted that the sky was gloomy & gray every day. When we asked about it, we were told they were about to have a big storm. Not so much. We later found out it was just tons of pollution. Then we saw Xian in the West. The old capital where the Buddhist monk left from and returned to after he got back from India. A pagoda built for him and the scriptures he brought back is still standing. Just outside of town is the tomb of one of the first emperors. Over 2000 years ago he buried a massive army of terra cotta soldiers with him. Each one is slightly different. Pretty impressive.

From there we flew to the Yangtze River just as they were finishing the 3 Gorges Dam that would eventually flood thousands of homes to make the river more navigable and make electricity. As it was being built, cracks were already appearing. Hopefully they have fixed it by now. We took a slow ride up river to Chongqing. On the boat they offered Tai Chi classes in the mornings. It is somewhat similar to yoga but moves a lot slower and is less demanding. Too much of both for me, but it seems to give the same mental & physical benefits as yoga while being easier to do. They also had a Chinese medicine doctor on the boat rather than a Western one. She even gave us a few lectures on Chinese medicine & acupuncture. While there we saw pandas & a memorial to the American fighter pilots who were stationed there in WW2. We also saw our tour bus driver go the wrong way on the freeway and later come within inches of sideswiping another car. There is some truth to the stereotype about Asian drivers, it seems. But when an entire country starts to drive in a matter of a few years for the first time in their lives, what do you expect? And our bus driver was a professional driver. Imagine how good the amateurs are.

From there we went to Shanghai. While there is a part of Beijing with some modern buildings and almost Vegas level lights, Shanghai has an area that is THE most modern and experimentally designed place I have ever seen. It almost looks like something from a science fiction movie. We went to a hospital there called something like the Chinese-Japanese Friendship Hospital. Guilty conscience from WW2? It was unlike any Western hospital in one big way. When someone checked in at the front desk, they were quickly assessed and sent to the Western Medicine side for standard medical care or to the Traditional Chinese Medicine side for acupuncture, herbs, etc.

While acupuncture and Chinese herbal medicines can work and potentially are better than Western medicine for some things; the problem is that nearly no modern scientific studies have been done to see how or if most of them work. The Chinese use an old pre-scientific way of explaining disease and treatment that focuses on hot vs. cold and wet vs. dry. They even 'locate' it to various regions like 'the liver'. Of course, there is about as much real support for this as Hippocrates breaking disease down to imbalanced 'humors'. Acupuncture itself does have a 'map' of the various pressure points and energy (chi) channels that pretty closely tracks with the layout of the nerves in the body and their switching stations (ganglion). It has been shown on brain scans to affect the level of various neurotransmitters. Too much of Chinese medicine though is based on superstition. A basic principal of magic is: like causes like. Despite this nobody is ever going to convince me that powdered rhino horn or tiger penis is better than Viagra. At least not any more than they are likely to convince me to put leeches on my patient because they have 'too much blood humor'.

My second trip was just last year. This time we went to 2 much less popular places in the south, Nanning & Xiamen. Most foreigners, including myself (& I'm pretty informed about China) have never even heard of Nanning. I got really lucky; a friend of a friend knew someone at the medical school in Nanning. They were having an international Critical Care Medicine conference there and they had a last-minute cancellation of a lecturer from the US. Since I speak reasonable Chinese and like to travel, my friend asked me if I wanted to give a lecture in China, all expenses paid & a little extra $ as a speaker fee. I of course said 'Hell YES!' I found out there that they advertised the conference as having speakers from China & several other countries including the US. As there was only 1 speaker scheduled from the US, it was easy to see why they were so eager to get me there when the original speaker dropped out.

During the entire trip, even counting the airports since we flew with a small regional Chinese airline, we saw at most a dozen White people from the moment we got on the plane. Southern China is tropical and green, quite a contrast from the often dry, desert-y North. This means the food is different of course. The famous Dim Sum brunch type food comes from the South. It also seems to be reflected in the overall feel of the people. They seem more relaxed and friendly in the South, but much less likely to speak English. Even the sky was clear. Maybe this is because they are farther from the big economic and tourist centers. Maybe this is just the effect of 13 years of further development, pollution control and opening to the West since my last trip. Since I was there before, the Chinese have gotten their own electric car company & have mandated that all motorbikes be replaced by electric ones. They have also gotten serious about global warming, unlike us lately (Thank You Wittle Donnie Trump!). Maybe it's something like the carefree, relaxed stereotype of people in warm climates, like they talk about in Southern Europe or the Southern US for that matter. Maybe just that we were not part of a big tourist group and were honored guests. Either way, there was a noticeable change from my previous trip for the better.

Nanning is a small inland city by Chinese standards with *only* 7 million people. Like the new part of Shanghai 13 years ago, most of the new and bigger buildings now are hypermodern and alien looking. What's more, most of the newer buildings are lit up from top to bottom at nite. More often than not with moving scenes or shows. While this would be tacky as hell if done in Vegas, it really works there. Xiamen is a charming seaside city that is much more traditional. There are a few beautiful Buddhist temples. The bigger one is a lot more popular. The other is actually a group of 2 or three temples at different levels of a hill. The view from the top gives a view of the entire city. Xiamen faces Taiwan and you can even see it on a clear day from part of the city. As an example of the early Communist paranoia, locals were not allowed to go to the area where you could see Taiwan until relatively recently.

Both trips to China were wonderful experiences. After the first trip, especially after visiting other countries in the area, I was a little biased against returning to China. I had seen most of the 'good parts' & the North seemed like a giant master-planned community. The people weren't terribly friendly and didn't seem terribly happy either. My recent trip turned all that on its ear. This trip everything was different for the better.

I will never know how much of the difference was the South vs. the North, 13 years of development or me. Regardless, I am excited about China again & looking forward to my next trip.

THE GENTLEMAN

Gentleman Bank Robber: noun. An apparently somewhat common name for several different men & at least one lady bank robber. Given to them because they were polite &/or well-dressed during their hold ups.

-my conclusion/definition after a fruitless internet search for one particular GBR

The Gentleman was an older guy about 60 with crappy luck. **He** had breast cancer. Less than 1% of all cases of breast cancer are in men. Since cancer can cause weird clotting, it is a common cause of clots in your veins. These can travel up to your lungs and kill you if they are not treated. Most people get it in a leg or sometimes an arm & a piece may break off and go up to the lungs. His were filling up a lot of the veins in his chest. Medicines to break the clots up weren't working & his surgeon was talking about going in surgically and stripping them out last time I heard. With all he had going on, I saw him a lot in the ER and occasionally had to go upstairs at nite to take care of some issue he (or anyone upstairs had) since in small hospitals the ER doctor is normally the only doctor in house at nite. I got to know him reasonably well from all these visits, particularly because he was a perfect gentleman. Always nicely dressed and polite. Engaged in his care but realistic and reasonable about his disease. A smart, happy, interesting guy to talk to.

I also call him The Gentleman because of his former 'job'. He told me how for a while in the eighties or nineties, he was famous as the

Gentleman Bank Robber. I can easily believe it even though I have never been able to find him by looking on Google. It is surprising to me, at least, how many GBRs have existed. Who knew? Apparently, it is a cottage industry.

One of the last times we talked, we got around to how bad his luck was between the cancer and the clots.

Trying to provide some comfort, I told him the old saying: 'You have to play with the cards you are dealt'. True. And something he was already doing.

His reply was original and showed what a mature outlook he had: 'And you have to DEAL with the cards you PLAY'.

And he was dealing pretty damn well. I don't think I ever heard him truly complaining or having a (not unreasonable) meltdown or whatnot over his problems.

I am pretty sure he is no longer with us between all his issues and just the fact that a dozen years have passed in the life of an older guy.

I am also sure my buddy The Gentleman went out with his head held high, deservingly surrounded by his loved ones.

That's just how a Gentleman rolls …

THE HYENA

Hyena: Noun. A <u>dog-like African</u> mammal with forelimbs that are longer than the hind limbs and an erect mane. Hyenas are noted as scavengers, but most are also effective hunters.

-dictionary definition, underlining by me

There is an old saying in medicine: 'If you hear hoof beats, think horses before zebras'. It illustrates another old saying: 'Common things are common'. Despite learning all about those weird rare diseases in medical school, almost all patients will end up having more common problems. Not some weird disease found in 1.5 people per million or in 90% of Google searches to find out what your symptoms are from. As I tell my patients: 'Don't listen to Dr. Google. He is an idiot & they just took away the medical license he never had'. Catastrophic misdiagnoses can & do occur when doctors don't think of the weird, rare option; but not very often. Unless you are in Africa, the next hoof beats you hear are not likely to be from an escaped zebra from the zoo. And unless you are in Montana, the next hoof beats you hear are more likely from Youtube or Netflix anyway.

Dog bites are a perfect example of this. Most dog bites are probably from those vaguely dog-like inbred rat looking little things, but since pit bulls have such a bad reputation, about 90% of **reported** dog bites are 'from' pit bulls.

One female (definitely not lady) patient I had took this to the next level of crazy. But then she **was** bipolar, so crazy was the real answer.

209

I'm pretty sure **she** had rabies. At least she was more likely to have had it than the poor wittle doggie that bit her. I hope the dog had its shots, so it didn't get anything from her. She was practically frothing at the mouth and all over the place. But then bipolar does that.

And bipolars or schizophrenics are impossible to reason with after a certain point. It is not worth your time to even try. Anymore, when I start getting the crazy card from psych patients or drug addicts who are telling me impossible crap, I just try to tell them: 'No. That is not possible. No. I will not look at the conspiracy theory pic you shot on your phone. No. That is just your mental illness (&/or drugs) telling you that. No. We are not going to waste our time talking about that, any more than we are going to have a discussion about Santa Claus or the Easter Bunny'. Rarely works, but I would rather walk away & get the nurse to give them some anti-crazy medicine than keep trying to get the details of what is actually happening when all they want to talk about is the aliens who put a listening device up their butt.

One patient called 911 'because he was shot in the foot'. I don't work in a trauma center, so if it was real, he wouldn't have come to me. He was obviously just schizophrenic or bipolar. He had a blister on his foot. Probably from walking for hours in bad shoes with no socks. A very common thing in the homeless population (as 90% of the homeless are alcoholics, drug addicts or mentally ill) & a common reason they end up in the ER. This guy was saying how he was shot with a radioactive bullet and demanding we get a Geiger counter. He refused anything but that and walked out after I tried to talk sense into him & told him no.

Anyway, back to the rabid woman. She kept saying she was bit by a **hyena**. Since this was LA & a good hour from the zoo & she was crazy, not so likely. Being younger and more optimistic back then, I tried to reason with her to no avail. When I asked WHY she thought it was a hyena, her answer was: 'Because it was ugly!'

No.

The world doesn't work that way.

And I have actually seen hyenas in Africa. They are beautiful, proud looking animals. And nobody could mistake one for a dog.

If I went by her criteria, tons of people I see every day would be considered hyenas ...

CPSIA information can be obtained
at www.ICGtesting.com
Printed in the USA
LVHW021055041119
636249LV00002B/327